Self Learning Course in Astrology

(Based on Systems' Approach)

By:

V.K. Choudhry, MBA.
K. Rajesh Chaudhary, MBA.

Salient Features:

A Complete Book for Beginners and Advance Learners giving Fundamental Concepts, Predictive and Interpreting Techniques with case studies for Easy Comprehension and Understanding. Must for pursuing Predictive Accuracy. CASE STUDIES: *Analysis of Mental Capabilities, * Pre-marital Pleasures, *Marital Discord, & * How to Identify Heart Disease, Order of Significations.

Self Learning Course in Astrology

(Based on Systems' Approach)

Salient Features:

A Complete Book for Beginners and Advance Learners giving Fundamental Concepts, Predictive and Interpreting Techniques with case studies for Easy Comprehension and Understanding. Must for pursuing Predictive Accuracy.

CASE STUDIES: *Analysis of Mental Capabilities, * Pre-marital Pleasures, *Marital Discord, & * How to Identify Heart Disease, Order of Significations.

Author:

V. K. Choudhry

M.B.A., Founder Chairman,
International Institute of Predictive Astrology,
Fairfield, USA, and Propounder of Systems' Approach for Interpreting Horoscopes

Co-Author:

K. Rajesh Chaudhary

M.B.A., Vice President,
International Institute of Predictive Astrology, Fairfield, USA

Sagar Publications

72, Janpath, Ved Mansion, New Delhi-110001
Tel.: 23320648, 23328245
E-mail: sagarpub@vsnl.com
Website: www.sagarpublications.com

First Print 1992
Second Reprint 1994
Third Reprint 1996
Revised Reprint 1998
Reprinted 2001
Fourth Print 2004
Fifth Print 2007
Revised & Enlarged Edition 2013
Reprint 2017

Published and Printed by:
Saurabh Sagar for **Sagar Publications** New Delhi-110001

and

Printed at:
The Artwaves, New Delhi-110019, Telfax.: 41609709;
E-mail: theartwaves@gmail.com

ABOUT THE AUTHORS

Shri Vinod Kumar Choudhry

(Propounder of the Systems' Approach for Interpreting Horoscopes)

V. K. Choudhry

Shri V. K. Choudhry is well known in the field of Vedic Astrology through his many books and articles. His managerial background has enabled him to use modern communicative skills in so systematic a manner that the comprehension of predictive techniques has been greatly simplified. His book, "Self Learning Course in Astrology" makes learning of the "Systems' Approach" methodology a simple step- by-step process and has proved to be of great help to both the serious students as well as the practitioners still plagued by the confusing inconsistencies in the classical texts.

He was conferred the title of Jyotish Martund by the International Council of Astrological and Occult Studies, Hyderabad (India) in 1989; the title of Jyotish Kovid by the Indian Council of Astrological Sciences (ICAS), Madras, in 1991; and the title of Jyotish Bhanu by Astro Sciences Research Organization, New Delhi, in 1992. He has been a faculty member and Chapter Course Director (Astrology) with ICAS.

Shri Choudhry is the recipient of Pracharya Award (Professor of Astrology) conferred by Bharat Nirman in December, 1993, for his outstanding and excellent contributions in the field of Astrology.

In 1994, his name was listed in "Indo American Who's Who", in recognition of his contributions for predictive accuracy in Vedic Astrology.

Shri Choudhry participated in the 10th International Seminar of Astrology and Occult Science in June 1995, at Hyderabad and delivered lectures on "Timing of Events" and "Vastu Shastra". Shri Choudhry was conferred the title of "Master of Astrology" in this Seminar by the International Council of Astrological and Occult Studies.

The Board of Directors of the International Council of Alternative Medicines conferred the degree of Doctor of Alternative Medical Sciences on Shri Choudhry on the 3rd of February 1996, at Bombay. The International Institute of Astrology and Occultism, New Delhi, conferred a Gold Medal and the honorary title of Jyotish Vachaspathi on Shri Choudhry in April 1996, at New Delhi.

The International Foundation of Peace, Fraternity and Humanistic, Bombay, conferred the title of Dharam Yogi in 1995. The International Council of Astrological Sciences, Bombay, conferred the title of Vastu Shastra Samrat in 1996, and Bhartiya Ved Jyotish Vigyan Sansthan, Modinagar (India), conferred the title of Sthapatya Ratna in 1996, on Shri Choudhry for his valuable contributions in the fields of Astrology and Vastu Shastra. Shri Choudhry participated in astrological conferences in London, Paris and U.S.A. In 2004 the first book of Shri V. K. Choudhry was translated in Portuguese and published in Portugal. The Systems' Approach for Interpreting Horoscopes is applicable for Mundane Astrology predictions as well. Shri Choudhry has made many successful mundane predictions on Yahoo Groups – SAMVA, including twice predicting victory for Mr. George W. Bush as President of US, predicting a natural disaster for US in August, 2005, and predicting victory for Mr. Donald Trump as President of US in October, 2015.

The United Cultural Convention, North Caroline, USA, sealed the nomination of Shri V. K. Choudhry for receipt of the 2002 Noble Prize for Outstanding Achievement and Contributions to Humanity. This nomination stems from extensive research on extraordinary leaders by the top officials of the United Cultural Convention.

Shri Krishan Rajesh Chaudhary

K. Rajesh Chaudhary

Shri Krishan Rajesh Chaudhary has mastered and contributed to the Systems' Approach for Interpreting Horoscopes under the guidance of his father, Shri V. K. Choudhry. He participated in the free Consultation Clinics organized in New Delhi by Bharat Nirman in 1995-96. He is one of the Directors and Secretary of The Systems' Institute of Hindu Astrology, Gurgaon, India (SIHA). He is Vice-President of the International Institute of Predictive Astrology, Fairfield, USA. Delhi Astro Study Circle (Registered) New Delhi, conferred the honorary title of Jyotish Martund on Shri Chaudhary in 2011. The Indian Institute of Oriental Heritage, Kolkata, India, conferred the Life Time Achievement Award on Shri K Rajesh Chaudhary on 7th March, 2014. As a Secretary of SIHA he has been managing the presentations in the International Conferences of SA Astrologers in India since 2007. In December, 2014, the Tenth such Conference was held in Gurgaon.

He is the author of the following successful books:

1. Planets and Children
2. Impact of Rahu and Ketu
3. Financial Astrology

4. Methodology for Handling Astrological Studies

He is co-author for the following successful books:

1. Predictive Techniques and the Application of Astrological Remedial Measures.
2. Select Right Profession through Astrology.
3. A Complete Book on Medical Astrology.
4. A Complete Book on Horary Astrology.
5. How to Analyze Married Life.
6. Self Learning Course in Astrology.
7. How to Study Divisional Charts.
8. Triple Transit Influences of Planets
9. Interpreting Planetary Influences (System's Approach for Interpreting Horoscope).
10. Impact of Ascending Zodiac Signs
11. Jyotish Swayam Seekhiye (In Hindi).
12. Sagar's Daily Nirayana Planetary EPHEMERIES 2001-2025 (Based on Chitra Paksha/Lahiri Ayanamsa

Website: www.YourNetAstrologer.com
Website: www.JyotishRemedies121.com

SAGAR PUBLICATIONS

PREFACE

Astrology is an art of interpreting the reputed esoteric influence of stars/planets on human affairs. It is called the divine science. It enables one to peep into the mysterious future. It has many branches like horoscope reading, palmistry, transit, prasna, varshphala, etc. The most accurate and dependable one is the horoscope reading, which is linked to the birth time of the individual. In this system, the planetary position as at the time of birth is noted for interpreting the results of various aspects of life.

Astrology has its origin in the Vedas and is presently studied all over the world. There are different systems in operation and one of the best systems is the Vedic System of Astrology. In this system also there are number of sub-systems or schools of thought but the most time tested is the one given by Maharshi Parashara, especially when studied through the Systems' Approach (SA). There have been numerous commentators, both classical and modern and at the present juncture, the subject is being read by interested readers all over the world through the Parashari System. The comprehension of the system from the classical text is somewhat difficult and the attempt of the authors is to initiate the interested readers for easy comprehension of the subject.

The Vedic system of Astrology is based on the premise that the natal position of planets is dependent on the past karma (actions) of the human beings and gives complete picture of the life of the person concerned. It also believes that the horoscope/natal chart of the person tells us whether the malefic influences can be warded-off or reduced. It believes in strengthening of the weak planets to augment their better effects and to reduce the extent of miseries.

The interpretations are dependent on the position of planets in the heavens at the time of birth as well as at the time of interpretation. The positions as at birth are known as natal or radical positions while the positions at the time of interpretation on a subsequent date or dates are known as transit position of planets with reference to a birth chart.

Astrology is both a science and an art. It is a science as its principles of determining planetary positions and planetary periods are based on mathematical systems and even the predictive tools are universally applicable. It is an art to blend the numerous techniques available to an astrologer for predictions depending upon the place and time. The difference in opinion of various astrologers is because of the difference in comprehension, analytical approach and expression power of the different individual astrologers.

Scope of the Book

The scope of the book is to enable the readers to:

- Comprehend concepts of Astrology;
- Comprehend terminology of Vedic Astrology and Systems' Approach for Interpreting Horoscopes;
- Introduce you to fundamentals of interpreting a chart;
- Sharpening predictive skills of learners through case studies.

Structure

The system has two parts: (1) drawing a horoscope; and (2) interpreting the same. The concepts and fundamental principles will be taken up first so that you can comprehend the system in an interesting way. You can draw the birth chart through the software Jyotish Tools available from www.JyotishTools.com This makes your learning fast and accurate.

After you have gone through this book thoroughly and have comprehended the various concepts and the fundamentals of the Systems' Approach, you can proceed further for an advanced study of the system through the following books of authors for learning and mastering the art of predictions:

1. **Interpreting Planetary Influences (Systems' Approach for Interpreting Horoscopes).**

   FIFTH REVISED EDITION - RENAMED 2015

   Unique features are:

   *Latest Predictive Techniques

   *How to Identify the Results of *Placement of Planets

   *Delineating debilitated planets

   *Delineating significations of each house

   *Remedial measures

   How to Read the Chart of Twins

   Initiation of Remedial Measures

   Calculation of Strength of Planets

2. **How to Study Divisional Charts**

   Unique features are:

   - Use of Divisional Charts relative to Rasi
   - Analysing Debilitated Planets
   - Analysing Combust Planets
   - Ketu Dasa
   - Case studies using various Divisional Charts
   - Discussion of Vargottama planets, exalted planets, etc.

3. Impact of Ascending Zodiac Signs

Unique features are:

- How to analyse a horoscope in 3 minutes
- Description of persons born under each ascendant
- Suggested use of astral remedies for each ascendant
- Reasons for troubles to those with Taurus, Virgo, or Pisces ascendant

4. Triple Transit Influences of Planets

(A Guide for Studying Transit Influences)

Unique features are:

- Tips for Predictive Accuracy
- Rectification of Birth Charts (Through transit)
- An Illustration for Analysing results of Triple Transit in Chapter 12
- Dreaded Concepts of 'Manglik' and Sade Sati discussed
- Application of Remedial Measures
- Case Studies.

5. Predictive Techniques and the Application of Astrological Remedial Measures

Unique features are:

- Predictive Techniques
- Effects of evil lords and planets in malefic houses (dusthanas)
- Timing of events
- Recovery of patients
- Return of missing persons
- Financial prosperity
- Progeny problems

- Psychiatric problems
- Delay in marriage
- Early widowhood
- Criminal tendencies
- Relevance of Vastu
- Case studies

6. **A Complete Book on Medical Astrology**

   Unique features are:

   - Medical significations of planets, houses, and signs
   - Identifying health problems
   - Prime determinants of health
   - Timing recovery
   - Application of preventive astral remedies
   - Case studies

7. **Select Right Profession Through Astrology**

   Unique features are:

   - Identifying professional indications
   - Averting professional setbacks
   - Augmenting professional prosperity
   - Identifying level of status
   - Business enterprises and partnerships
   - Case studies

8. **How to Analyse Married Life**

   Unique features are:

   - Tips for spotting prominent events in life
   - Planetary configurations for marital happiness and discord
   - Astral remedies for solving marital problems
   - Special reference to most malefic influence

- Case studies: Delay and denial, lack of progeny, broken engagements, inharmonious relationships, divorce, death of spouse, harassment in marriage, extra-marital affairs.

9. **A Complete Book on Horary Astrology**

Unique features are:

- Concepts and Advanced Analytical Techniques
- Prime Determinants, Afflicting planets, Significators,
- Timing Events and Recovery
- Application of Preventive Astral Remedies
- Diverse Case Studies

10. **Planets and Children**

Unique features are:

- Timing of Birth of the Child
- Progeny Problems & Astral Remedies
- Care of the Newborn through Astrology
- Impact of Child Birth on Family
- Health of Child in Infancy
- Birth of Younger Siblings
- Talent of Child
- Education Prospects of Child
- Sports Talent
- Career Counselling for children
- Order of Seeing Significations

11. **Impact of Rahu and Ketu**

Unique features are:

- Role of Rahu and Ketu in Horoscope Analysis,
- Impact of Mysterious Rahu

- Results in the sub periods of Rahu
- Impact of Ketu
- How to analyze main period or dasha of Ketu
- Ascendant-Wise And House-Wise Impact of Natal/Transit Rahu & Ketu In a Horoscope
- Kalsarpa Yoga - The Myth and its Impact .....
- Case Studies:

  Vulnerabe Longevity, Delay in Marriage, Serious health problems, Denial of Marriage, Professional problems, Early death, Early death of husband, Addiction,Black Magic Apprehensions, Accidents, Critical Illnesses, Transits, Oath-taking Charts, etc.

12. **Financial Astrology**

    Unique features are:

    - Identifying Planetary Influences for Financial Resources,
    - Financial Significations of Houses and Planets
    - Predictive Techniques and Methodology
    - Mundane Astrology
    - Analyzing Financial Position
    - Role of Eleventh House
    - Results of Auspicious Combinations
    - How to Augment Financial Resources
    - Diverse Case Studies
    - Transit Significant Events
    - Concept of Marka Planet
    - Rationale of Astral Remedies
    - FAQs for Understanding of Predictive Techniques for all Aspects of Life.

13. Methodology for Handling Astrological Queries

Unique features are:

- Understanding planets in malefic houses
- Combust planets, Debilitation of planets
- Conjunction of Planets
- Making Predictions
- Divisional charts
- Ascendant-wise important aspects and Diverse Case Studies for making learning of handling Queries easy.

All the above books explain the subject through illustrative case studies for better comprehension of the Systems' Approach for interpreting horoscopes. We wish you a successful learning of the art of predictive astrology.

We sincerely thank the Editors of various astrological journals, who had been putting forward our views before the lovers of Astrology.

V.K. Choudhry
K. Rajesh Chaudhary

105, A-Block, South City- II
Gurugram (Gurgaon)-122018.
Ph. : 91-9811016333, 91-9899417444
E-mail: vkchoudhry@gmail.com
Website: http//www.YourNetAstrologer.com
http//www.JyotishRemedies121.com

CONTENTS

Chapter 1

Major Constituents of Astrology

The divine science of Astrology is a wonderful asset to the mankind. It unfolds the uncertainties in life, reduces tension, and enables one to move to the right direction. It deals with various aspects of human life such as health - physical and mental, business, social status, financial prosperity, name and fame, emotional stability, etc. The Predictive Astrology gives us the firm indications in life pertaining to the future events right at birth. At the same time, the astrological remedies help further by reducing the impact of malefic planetary influences. Astrology remedies also helps in harnessing the significations ruled by benefic planets in a nativity.

How do Planets Affect us?

The basis of astrology is Karma theory. Whatever we have to get or face in this life is based on the planetary influences arising in our horoscopes. The horoscope is map of the heavens (planets) in the twelve signs of zodiac placed in twelve number of houses. From this map of heavens we can read the planetary influences on human beings. We can also read the amount of free will which can be changed through astrology remedies. The strength of Sun, Mars, Jupiter and the lord of the third house or the planets in the third house show the magnitude of free will.

The world dreads today with the fear of AIDS, cancer, auto-immune disorders, cardiovascular diseases, psychiatric problems, etc. The modern system of medicine whether allopathic and/or alternative medicines offers us some guiding factors for preventing these dreaded diseases or early detection of these so that these can respond to symptomatic treatment. Astrology has the twin capacity to forewarn and forearm. The divine science of Astrology offers the preventive remedies for such diseases wherever the possibility of such a disease is indicated by the predictive capacity of Astrology.

We come across health problems even at birth time. The newborn individual concerned has no role to play in abuse of his/her food habits, etc. Astrology relates it to the deeds of the past life based on the theory of Karma. We are not trying to create here any orthodoxies or blind faith or fatalism. We are trying to share with you our experience of application of the principles of Astrology and astrology remedies in timing of the diseases and timing of recovery.

The timing is done with the help of the horoscope which is a record of the planetary position prevailing at the time of the birth of a particular person at a particular place. This is the most valuable gift of ancient knowledge to the mankind. All sciences depend on the experience by way of observations and analysis of hypothesis developed based on these observations. It is really painful when such a useful gift to mankind is just termed as a superstition without even a trial by the so-called rationalists.

Despite the phenomenal growth in the modern healing sciences, the permanent cure for the functional health problems, be it in the fields of psychological problems, cardiovascular problems, renal problems, asthmatic problems, liver problems, immunization power of the body, auto-immune disorders, cancer, etc., has not been found. Astrology offers us the preventive diagnostic power and the astral remedies - for preventive as well as helping curative measures. Administering medicine is supported manifold when combined with the astrology remedies. The planetary periods operating (sub-periods) read in conjunction with the transit influences indicate the time frame for recovery. This in turn gives patience and results of the symptomatic treatment both to the doctor and the patient.

The divine science of Astrology has four major constituents / elements. These are signs, houses, planets and planetary periods. It will be in the fitness of things if the four constituents of the system are briefly discussed for developing the understanding for learning the System of Astrology.

A. Signs

The first constituent of the System is signs. They are twelve in number and are ruled by the planets indicated against each of them:

	Signs		**Lords**	
1	Aries	(Mesha)	Mars	(Mangal)
2	Taurus	(Vrishabha)	Venus	(Shukra)
3	Gemini	(Mithuna)	Mercury	(Budha)
4	Cancer	(Karka)	The Moon	(Chandra)
5	Leo	(Simha)	The Sun	(Surya)
6	Virgo	(Kanya)	Mercury	(Budha)
7	Libra	(Tula)	Venus	(Shukra)
8	Scorpio	(Vrischika)	Mars	(Mangal)
9	Sagittarius	(Dhanu)	Jupiter	(Guru)
10	Capricorn	(Makara)	Saturn	(Sani)
11	Aquarius	(Kumbha)	Saturn	(Sani)
12	Pisces	(Mina)	Jupiter	(Guru)

The words within parenthesis indicate their nomenclature in Sanskrit. You will observe that the planets Mars, Venus, Mercury, Jupiter and Saturn rule over two signs. These planets have special attention to one of their signs and this sign is known as their mooltrikona sign. The mooltrikona signs of planets are as under:

1	Mars	Aries
2	Mercury	Virgo
3	Venus	Libra
4	Jupiter	Sagittarius
5	Saturn	Aquarius

The signs possess the positive and negative aspects of their lords according to their nature and strength. The most important quality is that they lead us to infer the extent of fructifications of the significations of a particular house. For example, if the sign Libra falls in a house and its lord Venus is in full strength, the significations of that house in particular will flourish to a very affluent level of the society in which a particular native (person) is living. The significations of various signs have been detailed in Chapter 4.

B. Houses

The second constituent of the System is houses. The houses are twelve in number. Each of the twelve houses of the horoscope deals with specific significations. The significations of the houses fructify under the planetary periods (sub-periods) connected with them. The significations of the houses have been detailed in Chapter 5. The houses are good and bad. The sixth, eighth and twelfth houses are known as bad (malefic) houses as these rule diseases, obstructions and losses, respectively.

C. Planets

The third constituent of the System is planets. In Vedic Astrology we consider the Sun, the Moon, Mars, Mercury, Jupiter, Venus, Saturn, Rahu and Ketu as planets. The Sun and the Moon are the luminaries. Rahu and Ketu are the shadowy planets. As the planets Pluto, Neptune and Uranus neither have a lordship over a house nor have a planetary period of their own, we do not consider them in the Predictive Astrology techniques.

The planets signify various things including the specific body parts and the functional system of health. For example, the Sun is personified as a king in the planetary cabinet. Persons having the Moon, the significator of mind, in the sign of the Sun would have the mental frame of enjoying life like a king i.e. of thinking big. The Sun signifies father, husband and male children. The Sun also rules heart, digestive system and vitality. The Moon rules the lungs, fluids in body, lymphatic system, etc. The significations of the planets have been detailed in Chapter 6.

Additionally, the planets govern the houses in a nativity where their mooltrikona signs fall. For example, if sign Libra falls in the eighth house, Venus would rule the significations of the eighth house.

The planets attain benefic or malefic functional nature in a nativity (horoscope) based on the lordship of benefic or malefic houses containing mooltrikona signs. The planets may be weak or strong. The functional malefic planets when influencing other planets or houses cause afflictions to them.

D. Planetary Periods

The fourth constituent of the System is planetary periods. Though various types of planetary periods for specific planetary combinations are mentioned in classical texts, we will consider only Vimsottari dasa system in this book as this is universally applicable for all sets of combinations in a nativity. Based on the longitude of the Moon in the natal charts, we calculate the operational major period of a particular planet and the balance period yet to be operational. The mater has been further elaborated in Chapter 7.

According to their strength in a horoscope, the planets give results of the general and particular significations ruled by them in their sub-periods. More light on this will be thrown at other appropriate places in the book.

Reasons for Problems in Life

1. Weak planets;
2. Badly placed planets;
3. Afflicted planets;
4. Prolonged transit affliction to weak natal planets;
5. Transit of slow moving planets - Rahu, Ketu, Jupiter and Saturn in malefic houses;
6. Sub periods of functional malefic planets.

How to Identify Planetary Influences in a Horoscope

1. Placement of planets;
2. Close conjunction of planets with other planets;
3. Close conjunction of planets with most effective point of houses;
4. Close aspects with other planets;
5. Close aspects with the most effective point of houses.

Chapter 2

Important Terminology

In this chapter you will be introduced to the terminology of Astrology to enable you to comprehend the system. The Astronomy relevant to Predictive Astrology will be discussed in the first place.

Astronomical Terminology

Even if you find it difficult to understand astronomical terms, you can proceed with further study. The lack of clear understanding of the astronomical terminology will not create hurdles in your understanding of the Predictive Astrology. Predictive Astrology and Astronomy are two different sciences. Predictive Astrology is based on Astronomy but the deep knowledge of Astronomy is not at all necessary for predictive analysis.

Ecliptic

Ecliptic is the apparent path of the Sun.

Zodiac

Zodiac is an imaginary belt in the heavens extending to 9° on both sides of ecliptic containing 12 signs of 30° each. The first sign starts from 0° of the sign Aries (Mesha) and extends to 30°. Each degree can be divided into 60 minutes, and each minute can be divided into 60 seconds for the purpose of precision in calculations. The significations of the signs have been elaborated in seriatim in Chapter 4.

From the earth, the signs appear to be moving in a clockwise motion. The earth has two revolutions: one around the Sun which is completed in 365.25 days. The other revolution is around its own axis which is completed in 24 hours. Due to earth's movement around the Sun, when the Sun is viewed in the background of the zodiac it appears from the earth that the Sun moves/rotates at the speed of 1° per day in an anti-clockwise direction. The other revolution of the earth i.e. around its own axis causes rise of all the 12 signs in the horizon or east in a period of 24 hours.

The zodiac is also divided into 27 nakshatras (constellations) consisting of groups of fixed stars. The names and extent of nakshatras in zodiac are being separately indicated in the table appended at the end of the book.

Equinox

Equinox is the time when the Sun apparently crosses the equator and the day and the night are equal. It is believed that when the Sun touches its equinoctial point of zero degree of Aries, the earth moves westward with reference to a particular constellation. The zodiac seen or measured from the beginning of Aries from the westward moving equinoctial point is known as moving or tropical zodiac. When zero degree of Aries is reckoned from a particular star, the same is known as fixed or sidereal zodiac. The Sun enters Aries almost on identical dates every year. In the Vedic system of Astrology, when we are speaking of various signs we are actually speaking about the fixed constellations with the same name. The Vedic system of Astrology is known as Nirayana System.

Ayanamsa

Western astrology uses the concept of fixed zodiac while Vedic astrology uses the concept of moving zodiac. The moving zodiac gives a difference of about 56 seconds per year and this difference is known as Ayanamsa. The present value of this Ayanamsa is about 24.03 degrees. In Vedic Astrology this 24.03 degrees difference is subtracted from the apparent longitude of the planet which places the planet in a house prior to as indicated in the Western astrology, in some cases. Vedic Astrology gives better reading of planetary influences.

Solar Time

We measure time based on the concept of the solar day. It is defined as an average time period of the successive passages of the Sun over a given meridian. It is exactly 24 hours and is known as the mean solar day.

Sidereal Time

The time required for a 360 degree rotation of the earth around its axis, causing a given star in the sky to return to the same position in relation to the earth is known as the sidereal day and this period is about 23 hours, 56 minutes and 4 seconds.

Planetary Longitudes

Planetary longitude is the angular distance measured eastward on the ecliptic from the starting point of the fixed zodiac and it gives the apparent position of the planet in a particular sign at a given time.

Longitude

Longitude is the angular distance of any place on the earth's surface, east or west of a standard meridian (e.g. that of Greenwich), measured in degrees up to 180° east or west, or in units of time (1 hour = 15°). With the help of the longitude of a particular place with reference to Greenwich (0°), we calculate the local mean time for that place. As the earth rotates from west to east (anti-clockwise), those places east of Greenwich will be ahead of Greenwich Time and those to the west will be behind Greenwich Time. For each degree of longitude, there is a difference of four minutes in time.

Latitude

Latitude is the angular distance on its meridian of any place of the earth's surface from the equator. It is measured in degrees and minutes from the equator towards either the North Pole or the South Pole. The equator represents 0 degree latitude. Latitudes are thus lines drawn parallel to the equator.

Astrological Terminology in Systems' Approach

In this chapter we will introduce you to the terminology of Systems' Approach Astrology to enable you to comprehend the system.

Natal Chart

Natal chart or radical chart or horoscope or natal positions are the positions of the ascendant and planets in various signs as noted for the time of the birth. Natal positions, therefore, are fixed. The planetary positions noted with reference to a particular chart for subsequent periods are known as transit or transit positions.

Conjunction

Conjunction is the apparent coincidence or proximity of two or more celestial objects as viewed from the earth. The conjunction can be exact or close. If the difference in longitudes happens to be less than one degree, the resulting conjunction is known as an exact conjunction. If the difference in longitudes is within five degrees, the same is known as a close conjunction.

Example Chart 1

This example is given for clear understanding of the exact or close conjunctions.

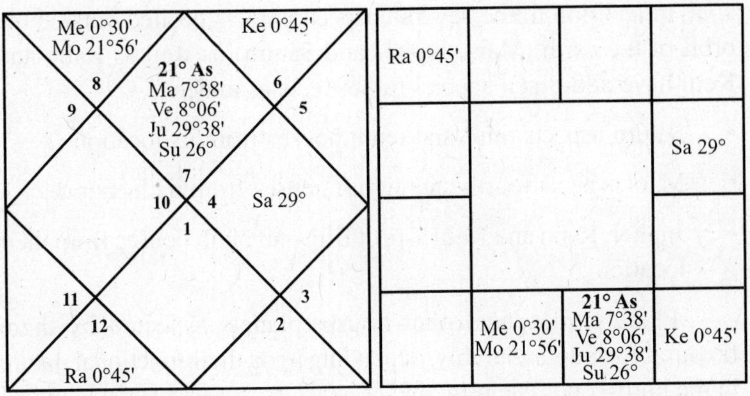

Me 0°30'
Mo 21°56'
21° As
Ma 7°38'
Ve 8°06'
Ju 29°38'
Su 26°
Ke 0°45'
Sa 29°
Ra 0°45'
1 2 3 4 5 6 7 8 9 10 11 12

Ra 0°45'			
			Sa 29°
	Me 0°30' Mo 21°56'	21° As Ma 7°38' Ve 8°06' Ju 29°38' Su 26°	Ke 0°45'

In this chart the planets Venus and Mars are in exact conjunction in the ascendant as their longitude difference is less than one degree.

The planets Sun and Jupiter are in close conjunction as their longitude difference is within five degrees.

The Moon is in exact conjunction to the most effective point of the second house.

Though Jupiter and Mercury are in the first and second houses, respectively, but they are in exact conjunction as their longitude difference is within one degree.

Aspects

The aspects are partial and full. In the Vedic system of Astrology, we are concerned with only full aspects. Each planet is believed to aspect fully the seventh house, reckoned / counted from the placement of the former.

In addition to the seventh aspect, planets posited outside the orbit of the earth (Mars, Jupiter and Saturn) as well as Rahu and Ketu have additional special full aspects as under:

- Saturn aspects third and tenth houses from its location.
- Mars aspects fourth and eighth houses from its location.
- Jupiter, Rahu and Ketu aspect fifth and ninth houses from their location.

Planets influence other houses/planets aspected by them favourably or unfavourably, depending upon their functional nature in the horoscope. The principle of exact or close aspect is identical to exact or close conjunction i.e. when a planet casts its aspect on another planet(s) or on the most effective point of house(s) within an orb of one degree, the aspect is known as an exact aspect. If the difference in planetary longitudes is within five degrees, then the aspect is known as a close aspect.

Example Chart 2

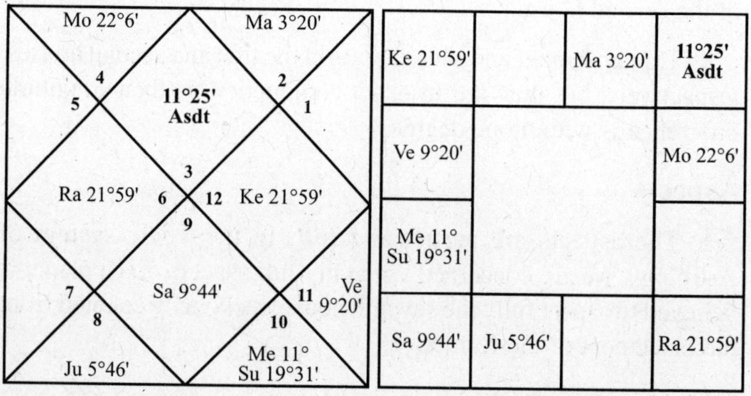

Mo 22°6'
Ma 3°20'
4
2
5
11°25'
Asdt
1
3
Ra 21°59'
6
12
Ke 21°59'
9
7
Sa 9°44'
11
Ve
9°20'
8
10
Me 11°
Su 19°31'
Ju 5°46'

Ke 21°59'		Ma 3°20'	**11°25' Asdt**
Ve 9°20'			Mo 22°6'
Me 11° Su 19°31'			
Sa 9°44'	Ju 5°46'		Ra 21°59'

This example is given for clear understanding of the exact or close aspects.

In this chart the planet Rahu closely aspects the Sun with fifth aspect as the longitude difference is less than five degrees.

The planets Mars and Jupiter mutually form close aspect as their aspect longitude difference is within five degrees.

Mercury forms exact aspect to the most effective point of the second house. This is the seventh aspect of Mercury.

Ketu forms exact aspect to the Moon placed in the second house. This is fifth aspect of Ketu to the Moon from the tenth house.

Saturn forms exact aspect to Venus as the longitude difference is less than one degree between the longitude of the two planets. This is third aspect of Saturn from seventh house to Venus placed in the ninth house.

Saturn forms close aspect to the most effective point of the ascendant as the longitude difference is less than five degrees between the longitude of Saturn and the ascendant. This is seventh aspect of Saturn from the seventh house to ascendant.

Wide Conjunction or Aspects

The conjunctions or aspects with more than five degrees of longitudinal difference are wide conjunctions or aspects. These do not have permanent impact in life except the short lived transit influences on the planets involved in wide conjunctions or aspects. The wide aspects give their results in later part of life, say around 60 years or after.

The aspect of a functional benefic planet will be effective corresponding to the strength of the planet(s)/house(s) involved. If the aspecting functional benefic planet is weak due to any reason including debilitation its effectiveness will be weak and limited, but its close aspect will always act as a helping force. The close aspect of a functional malefic planet, except on the most effective point of its mooltrikona house, will always act as a damaging force.

General and Particular Significations of Planets

The general significations of a planet mean the aspects ruled by that planet. For example, the Sun rules father, status of the person, job, heart, digestive system, etc., irrespective of the lordship of the Sun in a particular birth chart.

The particular significations of a planet mean the significations of its mooltrikona sign house in the natal chart. If the sign Leo rises in the third house then the Sun will rule the third house. The significations of the third house will be known as particular significations of the Sun.

The results of the significations of a weak planet fructify with delay and suffer whenever that weak planet is afflicted due to close aspect or conjunction with any functional malefic planet. The natal affliction causes damages in the entire sub-periods of the weak planet and the afflicting planets. The transit affliction causes short term damages during the effective transit influence.

Planetary States

The planetary states are the conditions in which a planet is placed. The prominent states and the results produced are as under:

1. **Infancy:** Whenever the longitude of a planet in a particular sign is less than 5 degrees, it is said to be in infancy. Such a planet is incapable of fully promoting/ protecting its general and particular significations.

2. **Old Age:** Whenever the longitude of a planet in a particular sign is more than 25 degrees, it is said to be in old age. Such a planet is incapable of fully promoting/ protecting its general and particular significations.

3. **Own Sign:** A planet in its own sign is treated as strong and is capable of generating the expected results, provided it is otherwise strong and is a functional benefic planet.

The own signs of various planets are as under:

Planet	**Own Sign**
Sun	Leo
Moon	Cancer
Mars	Aries, Scorpio
Mercury	Gemini, Virgo
Jupiter	Sagittarius, Pisces
Venus	Taurus, Libra
Saturn	Capricorn, Aquarius

4. **Mooltrikona Sign:** A planet in its mooltrikona (MT) sign is treated as very powerful, provided it is otherwise strong.

   Under the Systems' Approach, the mooltrikona signs of various planets are as under:

Planet	**Mooltrikona Sign**
Sun	Leo
Moon	Cancer
Mars	Aries
Mercury	Virgo
Jupiter	Sagittarius
Venus	Libra
Saturn	Aquarius

5. **Exaltation:** The planets are in exaltation in particular signs and give good results by promoting/protecting their general and particular significations, provided they are otherwise strong.

The exaltation signs of various planets are as under:

Planet	**Exaltation Sign**
Sun	Aries
Moon	Taurus
Mars	Capricorn
Mercury	Virgo
Jupiter	Cancer
Venus	Pisces
Saturn	Libra
Rahu	Taurus
Ketu	Scorpio

6. **Debilitation:** The planets are in debilitation in particular signs. The debilitated planets become weak and fail to fully protect/ promote their general and particular significations. Rather, there can be deterioration in their ruling sub-periods.

   The debilitation signs of various planets are as follows:

Planet	**Debilitation Sign**
Sun	Libra
Moon	Scorpio
Mars	Cancer
Mercury	Pisces
Jupiter	Capricorn
Venus	Virgo
Saturn	Aries
Rahu	Scorpio
Ketu	Taurus

7. **Combustion:** Whenever a planet comes very near to the Sun, it is divested of its brightness (lustre). The said state is called combustion. While in combustion, the planets fail to fully protect/promote their general and particular significations. If such a planet is weak on other accounts too, the significations ruled by them do not even take birth.

   The planets are said to be combust when they are within the below mentioned degrees on either side of the Sun:

Moon	12	Degrees
Mars	17	Degrees
Mercury	14	Degrees
Venus	10	Degrees
Jupiter	11	Degrees
Saturn	15	Degrees

8. **In Friendly Signs:** When planets occupy the signs of their friendly planets, they are happy and feel themselves free for producing results, if they are otherwise strong. The Sun, the Moon and Mars are friends and Jupiter is their preceptor. Saturn, Mercury, Rahu and Ketu are friends and Venus is their preceptor.

9. **In Inimical Signs:** When planets occupy signs of their enemies, they do not find themselves comfortable to produce results expected of them. However, any sign from where a particular planet aspects its own mooltrikona sign is an exception to this rule and a planet in such a state does not find itself restricted to produce results.

Chapter 3

Introduction to Charts

Ascendant / Lagna / Rising Sign

The revolution of the earth around its own axis causes rise of all the twelve signs in the east at different points of time during the period of 24 hours in a clock-wise motion. The signs rise in seriatim i.e. Aries first, and then Taurus followed by Gemini and so on and so forth.

The ascendant or lagna is that point in the zodiac which rises at the time of birth of a person with reference to the place of birth. The position of planets in zodiac is noted with reference to the earth. The ascendant is the first house in a horoscope and the rest of the houses are reckoned from it.

Rasi Chart/Natal Chart/Main Chart/ Horoscope

The rasi chart which is known as birth chart or natal chart can be drawn in many ways but for the purpose of our study, we will only take up north Indian type chart style as under:-

North Indian Chart Style

This is the best form of drawing a chart as it provides a very easy comprehension of the chart at a mere glimpse. It shows angles/ planets placed in angles without enumeration.

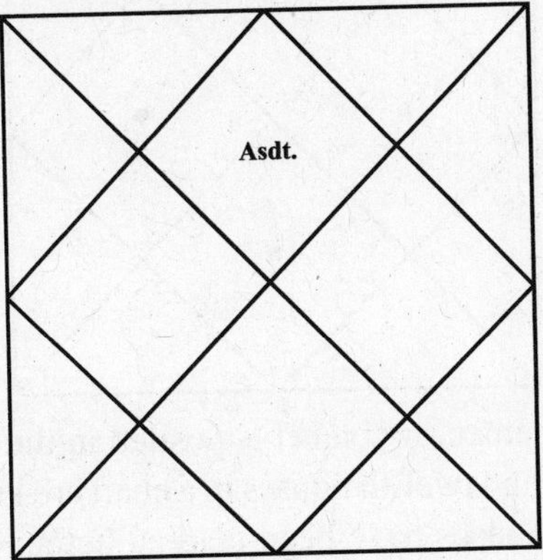

Even identification of the houses is very easy in this form of a birth chart. The houses are always fixed and are shown below:

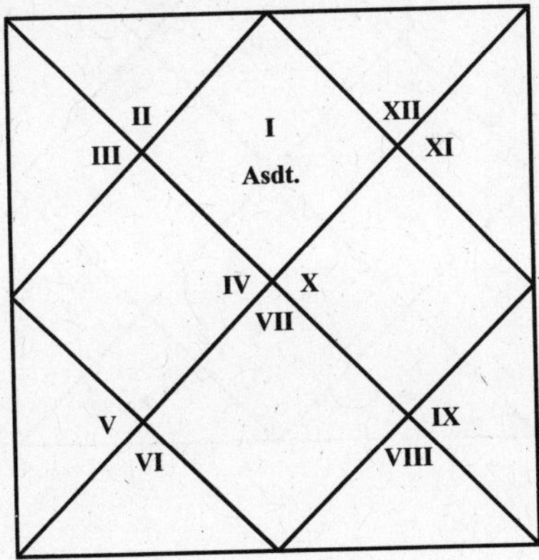

Angular houses have been marked hereunder:

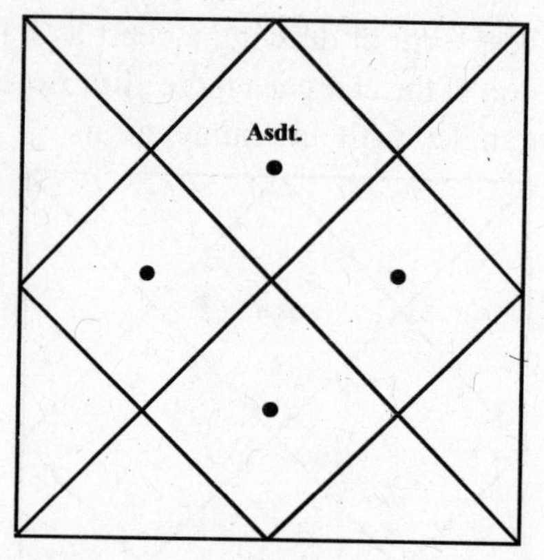

It shows whether any planet is posited in the malefic houses. The sixth, eighth and twelfth houses in a chart are known as malefic houses. Malefic houses have been marked hereunder:

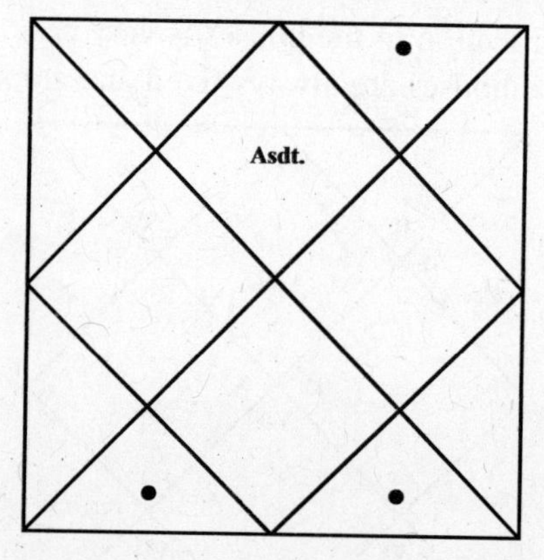

It shows the placement of planets in trines, if any, at a mere glimpse. The trinal positions have been shown as under:

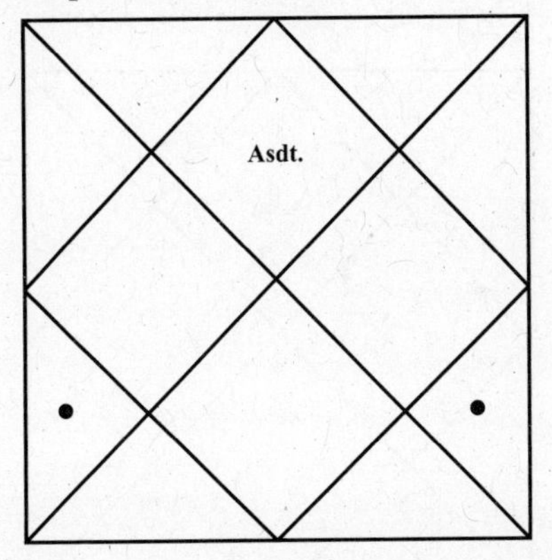

Even reckoning of the aspects is very easy in this form of a birth chart. The houses are always fixed and are shown below:

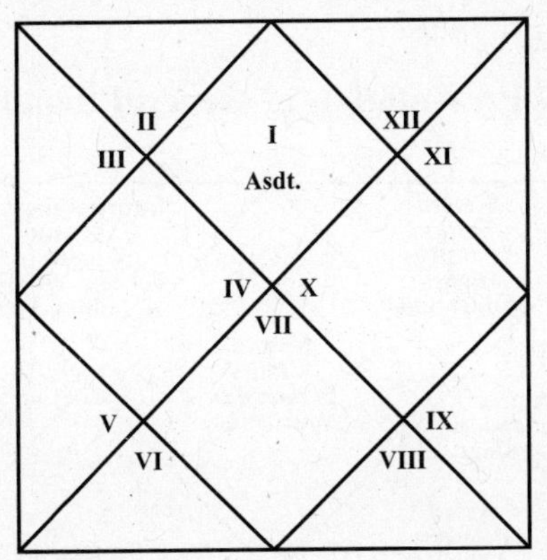

According with Systems' Approach, the lordship of the houses is reckoned from the placement of a mooltrikona sign in a particular house. The lord of the mooltrikona sign placed in a particular house is called the lord of the house. The counting of houses is done in an anti clockwise direction. In the following chart, for example, the sign Gemini rises in the ascendant:

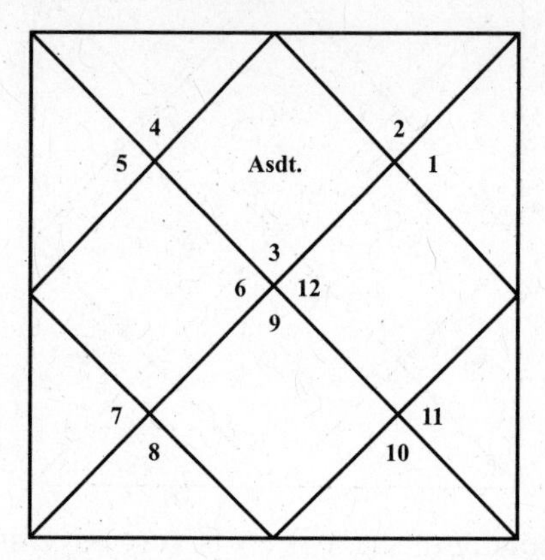

As the sign Libra is placed in the fifth house, Venus will be the lord of the fifth house.

Graphical Presentation of General Significations of the Houses

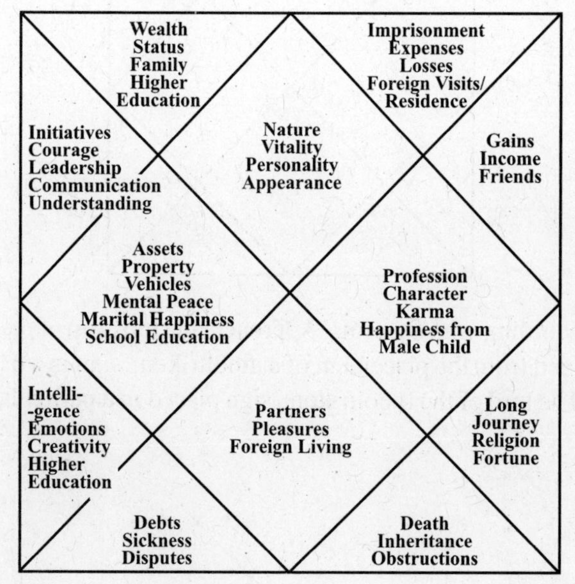

Graphical Presentation of Body Parts Ruled by the Various Houses

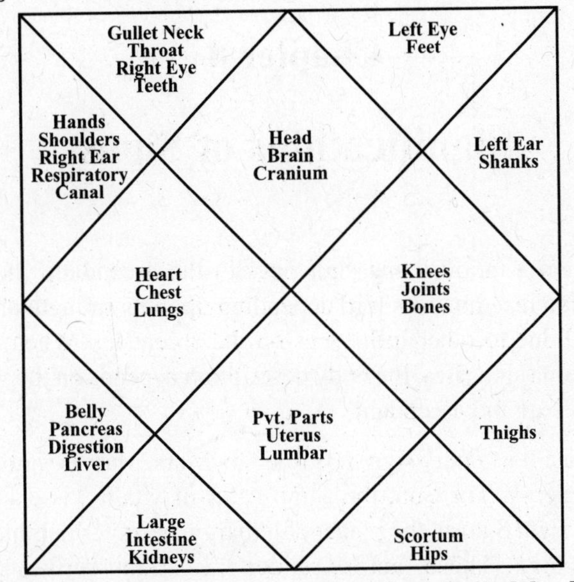

Graphical Presentation of Relations Ruled by Various Houses

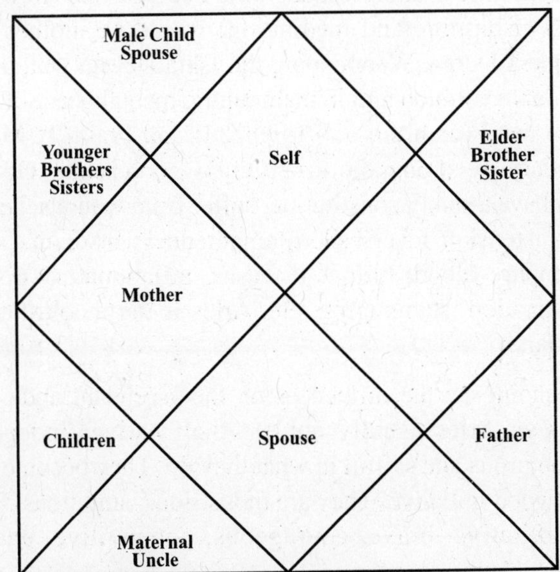

Chapter 4

Significations of Signs

When a mooltrikona sign rises in the ascendant, the body description resembles its lord depending upon its strength and gets modified due to other influences on the ascendant. When a non-mooltrikona sign rises, the body description depends on the various influences on the ascendant.

1. **Aries:** It is a fiery sign. It is ruled by Mars. Mars is significator of energy. The Sun, the significator of vitality, is exalted in this sign. Saturn, the planet of lethargy, becomes debilitated in this sign. These factors render the Arians active, strong, aggressive and healthy when Mars is strong in the birth chart. If Aries rises as the ascendant, the Ishta Devata (form of god for worshipping and meditation) would be mother divine, Goddess Durga. Worshipping the Ishta Devata would help in spiritual evolution and in maintaining mental peace. This sign rules head (cranium and forehead) and brain. If Mars and Mercury are strong, the Arians enjoy good health. Otherwise, they have a sickly constitution, suffer from wounds, headache, mental tension, fevers, short-temperedness, insomnia, diseases of impure blood, bilious diseases, inflammatory disorders, constipation, stammering, etc. Aries is the mooltrikona sign of Mars.

   Depending on the influences on the ascendant and/or Mars, the sign Aries usually renders their natives independent, adventurous and skilful in what they do. They become leaders with good initiative. They are industrious, ambitious, fighters, authoritative, brave, courageous, competitive, energetic, enterprising and strong-willed. If Mars is weak and under malefic influence, they become argumentative, offensive, impatient, irritable, impulsive and self-centered. If Aries rises as the ascendant, the influence of Saturn turns them towards construction and makes them entrepreneurs. They earn lot of wealth by persistent efforts. Depending upon the strength of Mars being prime determinant for profession, the Sun ruling intelligence and being general significator for success in profession and the Moon ruling education, Arians become commanders, executives, manufacturers, military and para-military forces, police, project erectors, surgeons, etc. The influence of other planets on the tenth, first or second houses changes the professional pursuits.

2. **Taurus:** It is an earthy sign ruled by Venus. Venus is significator for materialistic pursuits and comforts. The Moon, the significator for caring, tenderness and affluence, is exalted in this sign. Ketu, the significator of spiritual pursuits, is debilitated in this sign. These factors render the Taureans materialistic, caring and sensual. They enjoy comfort, beauty and luxury around them. If Taurus rises as the ascendant, the Ishta Devata (form of god for worshipping and meditation) would be Lord Vishnu. This sign rules face and its organs (nose, throat, mouth, teeth and eyes), neck, cervical region and bones, cerebellum and facial bones. If Venus, as lord of the sixth house, is strong the Taureans enjoy good health. If Venus is weak, those born in Taurus ascendant have a sickly constitution. They suffer from poor digestion, disorders of the throat, eyes, etc., and diseases mainly arising out of a weak venous system. Over-indulgence can be a cause for ill health.

   Depending on the influences on the ascendant, the sign Taurus usually renders their natives cautious, prudent, stable, enduring, fixed in their ways and gentle. They become good planners, good communicators, analytical, straightforward, persevering, refined, attractive, patient, romantic, kind, sentimental, devotional, charming when the Sun, Moon, Mercury and Saturn are strong in their birth chart. They become possessive, jealous, stubborn, obstinate, resentful, passionate, lethargic and pleasure seekers if the malefic planets form close influences in the birth chart. Depending upon the strength of Saturn being prime determinant for profession, the Sun ruling education and being general significator for success in profession and the Moon ruling entrepreneurial nature, Taureans become businessmen, designers, engineers, technocrats, administrators, industrialists, house keepers, etc. The influence of other planets on the tenth, first or second houses changes the professional pursuits.

3. **Gemini:** It is an airy sign. It is ruled by Mercury, the significator of communication and confidence. These factors render the Geminians with excellent powers of speech and communication. They have an energetic nature and are always looking for change. They have innovative approach to life. If the mind is turned inwards, the native has the ability to progress far in the spiritual field. If Gemini rises as the ascendant, the Ishta Devata (form of god for worshipping and meditation) would be mother divine, Goddess Lakshami. This sign rules ears, lower neck, shoulders, arms, hands, respiratory and nervous systems, bronchial tubes, bones of arms and hands. As both the ascendant and the sixth house do not contain a mooltrikona sign, the Sun, the significator for vitality, would be considered as the prime determinant of health for Geminians. If the Sun is strong, they enjoy good health. Otherwise, Geminians have a sickly constitution and suffer from hypertension, headaches, congestion and respiratory diseases, asthma, imbalances in the nervous system, depression which can result in partial paralysis, stammering, shoulder pain, etc.

   Gemini sign in ascendant gives an ambitious nature with imaginative ideas. They usually love knowledge and like much movement, change and initiative. Depending on the influences on the ascendant, the sign Gemini usually renders their natives with a sharp intellect and conscious mind, spontaneous, adaptable, analytical, educated, learned, helpful, with teaching abilities, humor, wit and imagination or talkative. When the planets Moon, Sun and Mercury are weak, those born in Gemini ascendant become nervous, restless, agitated and indecisive. Depending upon the strength of Mercury ruling education, the Moon being prime determinant for profession and the Sun ruling entrepreneurial nature and being general significator for success in profession, Geminians become accountants, auditors, advisors, authors, writers, communicators, business men, computer programmers, engineers, experts in analytical work, intellectuals, journalists, lawyers, poets, publishers, salesmen, secretaries, software engineers, state services, etc. The influence of other planets on the tenth, first or second houses changes the professional pursuits.

4. **Cancer:** It is a watery sign. It is generally weak as it is ruled by the Moon, which is changeable in nature and tender. Jupiter, the significator of knowledge and fortune, is exalted in this sign. Mars, the significator of energy, is debilitated in this sign. These factors render the Cancerians caring and nurturing, highly emotional, intuitive, gentle and considerate. If Cancer rises as the ascendant, the Ishta Devata (form of god for worshipping and meditation) would be Lord Shiva. This sign rules the rib cage, chest, heart, lungs and breasts. If the Moon and Jupiter are strong, the Cancerians enjoy good health. Otherwise, they have a sickly constitution and unpleasant appearance and suffer from mental maladies, physical ailments of breast, chest, heart and epigastric region, lymphatic and circulatory congestion, jaundice and other liver complaints, etc. Under the Systems' Approach, Cancer is treated as the mooltrikona sign of the Moon.

   Depending on the influences on the ascendant and/or the Moon, the sign Cancer usually renders their natives good hosts, capable of receptivity and adaptability, generous, peace loving, with humor, wit and imagination or overly emotional, sensitive, shy, moody, attached and dependent. As the Moon is of volatile nature and becomes weak quite often either in brightness or by going to malefic houses from the ascendant or by being in infancy or old age or by going to its sign of debilitation, either in rasi or in navamsa, or by occupying the mooltrikona sign of any weak planet, the Cancerians are changeable to inconstant in their behavior. Depending upon the strength of Mars and the Sun being prime determinants of profession and the Moon for a stable profession, Cancerians become administrators, public relations managers, healers, nurses, house keepers, hoteliers, restaurant owners, catering professionals, cooks, eating-establishment owners, professionals dealing with liquids, etc. The influence of other planets on the tenth, first or second houses changes the professional pursuits.

5. **Leo:** It is a fiery sign. It is ruled by the Sun, the significator of vitality, intelligence, male progeny, social status and magnificence. These factors render the Leos noble hearts, with good character and strong will power when the Sun and Jupiter are strong. If Leo rises as the ascendant, the Ishta Devata (form of god for worshipping and meditation) would be mother divine, Goddess Durga. This sign rules upper belly, stomach, spine, spinal cord, back, liver, gall bladder, spleen and pancreas. If the Sun is strong, the Leos enjoy good health. Otherwise, they are vulnerable to the diseases of heart, spine, back, bones, spleen, pancreas, liver, stomach, weak digestion, fevers, etc., and lack stamina and will power. This is the mooltrikona sign of the Sun.

   When rising in the ascendant with a strong Sun, Leo makes the person noble, generous and gives majestic appearance. They prefer to be the centre of attention. Depending on the influences on the ascendant and/or the Sun, the sign Leo gives intelligence, strong will, initiative, awareness of authority and decisiveness, making their natives visionary, patient listeners, rulers, aristocratic, persevering, dramatic and bold or authoritative, dominant and ambitious. When the Sun is weak the Leo born people become jealous, impatient, stubborn, demanding, irritable and impulsive. Mercury is prime determinant for professional affairs The Sun is general significator for success in profession. Venus rules entrepreneurial nature. Depending upon the strength of Sun, Mercury and Venus, Leos may join a high service in government which offers security and good income, may earn through entertainment, sport, medicine, speculation or scientific pursuits, or may head large organizations, becoming organizers, administrators, contractors, corporators, leaders, politicians, etc. They will like to be self employed and will not like subordination. The influence of other planets on the tenth, first or second houses changes the professional pursuits.

6. **Virgo:** It is an earthy sign. It is ruled by Mercury, the governor of nervous system. Mercury, the significator of analytical faculties, is exalted in this sign and Venus, the significator for materialistic pursuits and comforts, is debilitated. These factors render the Virgos a discriminating nature and deep sensuality. If Virgo rises as the ascendant, the Ishta Devata (form of god for worshipping and meditation) would be Lord Vishnu. This sign rules the waist, abdominal umbilical region, nervous system, small intestine, upper part of large intestine, appendix and kidneys. If Mercury and Saturn are strong, the Virgos enjoy good health. Otherwise, they become hypochondriac and are vulnerable to overexertion, nervous breakdown, appendicitis, constipation, etc. This is the mooltrikona sign of Mercury.

   When Mercury is strong, it gives the power of analysis and discrimination. Depending on the influences on the ascendant and/or Mercury, the sign Virgo usually makes their natives communicative, attractive, charming, prudent, cautious, protective, analytical, dependable, honest, truthful, practical, sincere and detailed or critical. If Mercury is weak and afflicted, Virgo born people become neurotic, distant, resentful, indecisive and nit pickers with a fault finding tendency. As Mercury transits in a band of 28 degrees on either side of the Sun, for quite some time in the year it remains combust and weak. Then it goes to its sign of debilitation once a year for about a month and goes to infancy and old age about twelve times a year besides coming under the close influence of Rahu, Ketu and other functional malefic planets in a natal chart. The usual weakness of Mercury makes Virgo-born people feel insecure in life. They are generally worried and need support for maintaining self-confidence. If natal Mercury is weak, the person has prominent veins, lacks witticism and has no charm. Depending upon the strength of Venus, the Sun and Mercury, Virgos become accountants, artists, craftsmen, draftsmen, teachers, mathematicians, engineers, traders, writers, etc. They will be good at jobs that involve detailed work. The influence of other planets on the tenth, first or second houses changes the professional pursuits.

7. **Libra:** It is an airy sign. It is ruled by Venus, the significator for materialistic pursuits and comforts. Saturn, the planet of hard work and discipline, is exalted in this sign and the Sun, the significator of vitality and status, is debilitated. If the Sun which rules the soul is involved in this sign which rules luxuries and pleasures, the spiritual development of the person is obstructed and that is why the Sun gets debilitated in this sign. If Saturn is placed in this sign it gets exalted because Saturn ruling working class occupies the sign of luxuries and pleasures. These factors render the Libras a magnetic personality, if Venus is strong. If Libra rises as the ascendant, the Ishta Devata (form of god for worshipping and meditation) would be mother divine, Goddess Lakshmi. This sign rules lumbar region and lumbar bones, skin, lower part of large intestine, bladder and inner sexual organs such as ovaries, uterus, testicles and prostate gland. If Venus is strong, the Libras enjoy good health. Otherwise, they are vulnerable to diseases connected with parts ruled by this sign, skin diseases, diabetes, venereal diseases, renal problems, urination problems, arthritis, gout pains, etc. This is the mooltrikona sign of Venus.

Libra signifies sense of justice, clarity, strong will-power, optimism and is highly sensitive. Depending on the influences on the ascendant and/or strong Venus, the sign Libra usually gives their natives a strong sense of harmony, justice, balance, charm and aesthetic sense. It makes them spontaneous, artistic, charismatic, harmonizing, humanitarian, independent, adaptable, idealistic, talkative, thinker and able of considering different aspects of standpoint and judgment. Depending upon the strength of the Moon, the Sun and Venus, Libras become actors, actresses, financial advisors, hoteliers, legal advisors, managers, musicians, physicians, etc. They like public professions. The influence of other planets on the tenth, first or second houses changes the professional pursuits.

8. **Scorpio:** It is a watery sign. It is ruled by Mars, the significator of energy. Ketu, the planet of secrecy and intuition, is exalted in this sign and the Moon, the significator of change and tenderness, is debilitated. These factors render the Scorpios intuitive and rigid. If Scorpio rises as the ascendant, the Ishta Devata (form of god for worshipping and meditation) would be Lord Shiva. This sign rules outer sexual organs, scrotum, rectum, anus and pelvic bones. If Mars, as lord of the sixth house, is strong the Scorpio enjoy fairly good health. The Scorpios are of short stature, well built and enjoy good health when Mars is strong. When Mars is weak, they have a sickly constitution and suffer from piles, fissure, urinary infections, boils, and operations, etc., in the parts ruled by Scorpio.

   Scorpio signifies severe sentiments. Depending on the influences on the ascendant, the sign Scorpio usually renders their natives determined, disciplined, self-restrained, fearless, persevering, energetic, intense, dynamic, decisive, self-centered, straightforward and tough or very sensitive, introverted, secretive, stubborn and ready to defend themselves. Depending upon the strength of the Sun and Jupiter, Scorpios become administrators, advocates, chemists, detectives, officers in the Armed Forces, policemen, politicians, surgeons, traders in metals and chemicals, etc. The influence of other planets on the tenth, first or second houses changes the professional pursuits

9. **Sagittarius:** It is a fiery sign. It is ruled by Jupiter, the significator of fortune and knowledge. These factors render the Sagittarians ambitious, eager to learn and with good judgment. If Sagittarius rises as the ascendant, the Ishta Devata (form of god for worshipping and meditation) would be mother divine, Goddess Durga. This sign rules hips and thighs, arterial system, nerves and ear/hearing. If Jupiter is strong, the Sagittarians enjoy good health. Otherwise, they are vulnerable to anemia, poor digestion, flatulence, disorders of liver/gall bladder, jaundice, high fevers, diabetes, rheumatism and troubles in hips and thighs, etc. The native may also face troubles due to his tendency to overindulge in food and drink. This is the mooltrikona sign of Jupiter.

   Sagittarius signifies impressive personality. The first half of Sagittarius is human and the second half is quadruped. Depending on the influences on the ascendant and/or Jupiter, the sign Sagittarius usually makes their natives nature lovers, goal-oriented, clever, generous, cheerful, quick-witted, organized, philosophical, self-righteous or nit pickers, impatient, easily irritated and impulsive. The persons born under this sign are best suited for training or advisory roles due to their pleasant nature and analytical bent of mind. Depending upon the strength of Mercury, Jupiter and Saturn, Sagittarians play advisory roles and become businessmen, trainers for jobs, financial advisors, lawyers, legal advisors, teachers, physicians, religious leaders, etc. The influence of other planets on the tenth, first or second houses changes the professional pursuits.

10. **Capricorn:** It is an earthy sign. It is ruled by Saturn, the significator of dutifulness and responsibility. Mars, the significator of energy and ambition, is exalted in this sign and Jupiter, the significator of fortune and knowledge, is debilitated. These factors render the Capricornians ambitious, hardworking and selfish if not having a spiritual practice. It is the sign of

practical realization. If Capricorn rises as the ascendant, the Ishta Devata (form of god for worshipping and meditation) would be Lord Vishnu. This sign rules knees and kneecaps, skin, bones and joints. As both the ascendant and the sixth house do not contain a mooltrikona sign, the Sun, the significator for vitality, would be considered as the prime determinant of health for Capricornians. If the Sun is strong, they enjoy good health. Otherwise, Capricornians have a sickly constitution and suffer from joint pains/inflammation, arthritis, general weakness, emaciated body, skin diseases and allergies, etc. The native may also have troubles resulting from over work and nervous disorders.

Capricorn signifies tact, cheating, lethargy and melancholic nature if Saturn is weak in the nativity. Capricorn rising gives good looks if Saturn is strong. The aspect of benefic planets to the ascendant provides charm to the personality. The negative influences on weak Saturn, as lord of the second house, gives an appearance of a person advanced in age, sunken eyes, wrinkled body, etc. Depending on the influences on the ascendant, the sign Capricorn usually combines diligence and commitment with flexibility and adaptability and renders their natives traditional, level-headed, cautious, thrifty, conservative, methodical, social, practical, with organizing ability, faithful, prudent, protective, dependable and persevering or selfish, rigid and resentful. Depending upon the strength of Venus, the Sun and Saturn, Capricornians become businessmen, agriculturists, lawyers, leaders, politicians, etc. They are careful with their money. The influence of other planets on the tenth, first or second houses changes the professional pursuits.

11. **Aquarius:** It is an airy sign. It is ruled by Saturn, the significator of dutifulness and responsibility. These factors render the Aquarians independent and prepared to go against the established ways of behavior, if they feel that in doing so they are morally correct. If Aquarius rises as the ascendant, the Ishta

Devata (form of god for worshipping and meditation) would be mother divine, Goddess Lakshmi. This sign rules shanks, calves, ankles, shin bone, blood circulation, etc. If Saturn and the Moon are strong, the Aquarians enjoy good health. Otherwise, they are susceptible to colds and infections, and suffer from fractures in lower legs, cancerous diseases and wounds, etc., in the parts ruled by Aquarius. Rheumatism and arthritis are also indicated with age. This is the mooltrikona sign of Saturn.

Aquarius signifies characteristics like honesty, ideals and sensitiveness, etc., according to the strength of its lord. The body description resembles Saturn i.e. long stature, thin body and with prominent veins if Saturn is strong. Depending on the influences on the ascendant and/or Saturn, the sign Aquarius usually makes their natives willing to serve, helpful, with initiative, persevering and concentrated in work, active, courteous, deliberate, full of new ideas, decisive, humane, industrious, intuitive, scientific, studious, sympathetic, talented and unconventional or stubborn, rigid and impractical. Depending upon the strength of Saturn, the Sun and Mars, Aquarians become industrialists, leaders of the underdog, servants, thinkers, writers, religious teachers, etc. The influence of other planets on the tenth, first or second houses changes the professional pursuits.

12. **Pisces:** It is a watery sign. It is ruled by Jupiter, the significator of fortune and knowledge. Venus, the significator for materialistic pursuits and comforts, is exalted and Mercury, the significator of intellect, is debilitated in this sign. These factors render the Pisceans romantic, imaginative, compassionate and generous. If Pisces rises as the ascendant, the Ishta Devata (form of god for worshipping and meditation) would be Lord Shiva. This sign rules feet and toes, lymphatic system, bones of the feet and toe. If the Sun, as lord of the sixth house, is strong the Pisceans are healthy. Otherwise, they have a sickly constitution, suffer from gout pains, joint pains,

and disorders related with blood circulation, lymphatic system, feet, toes, bones of the feet/toes, etc.

Pisces signifies enjoyments, sensitiveness, etc. Depending on the influences on the ascendant, the sign Pisces usually renders their natives gentle, cheerful, empathetic, caring, devoted to duty, emotional, enthusiastic, idealistic, impressionable, intuitive, with moral values, mystical, philosophical, sentimental and tolerant or timid, vulnerable, indolent and ease loving. Depending upon the strength of Jupiter, the Sun and Mars, the Pisceans join the professions of commerce, development, financial advisor, legal advisor, training, etc. The person rises well in his profession and is generous. The influence of other planets on the tenth, first or second houses changes the professional pursuits.

How to Analyse Characteristics

The placement of a significator in a moveable sign makes a person dynamic in nature. The placement of a significator in a fixed sign makes a person less flexible in approach. The placement of a significator in a dual or common sign makes a person of adjustable nature. Aries, Cancer, Libra and Capricorn are moveable signs. Taurus, Leo, Scorpio and Aquarius are fixed signs. Gemini, Virgo, Sagittarius and Pisces are common (dual) signs.

The placement of the significator in a fruitful sign indicates early gains while the placement of the significator in a semi-fruitful sign indicates slow gains. The placement of a significator in a barren sign indicates gains after lot of efforts.

Fruitful signs: Cancer, Libra, Scorpio, Sagittarius and Pisces.

Semi-fruitful signs: Taurus, Capricorn and Aquarius,

Barren Signs: Aries, Gemini, Leo, Virgo,

The fiery element makes the person energetic and agile. Aries, Leo and Sagittarius are fiery signs.

The earthy element makes the person a pleasure-seeker and persistently engulfed in materialistic pursuits. Taurus, Virgo and Capricorn are earthy signs.

The airy element makes the person a thinker, creative and spiritualist. Gemini, Libra and Aquarius and airy signs.

The water element makes the person an ease-lover and keeps him fully involved in worldly attachments. Cancer, Scorpio and Pisces are watery signs.

The positive element shows greater chance of success. All odd signs are positive signs and all even signs are negative signs.

The biped element makes the approach of a person humanistic in life and he is generous, helpful and respectful to others. Gemini, Virgo, Libra, Sagittarius and Aquarius signs are biped signs.

Some Other Characteristics of the Signs

Prishthodaya Signs

Aries, Taurus, Cancer, Sagittarius and Capricorn are signs that rise with their hind parts first. If a significator planet is placed in these signs and is an indicator of timing the event, it will cause the event early.

Sirshodaya Signs

Leo, Virgo, Libra, Scorpio, Gemini and Aquarius signs rise with their head first and indicate that normal time would be taken for the fructification of an event.

Ubhyodaya Signs

Pisces rises with both sides. The events are timed with the help of the strength of the planet in question and merely the placement of the planet in the sign Pisces does not make a difference.

Directions of the Signs

Aries, Leo and Sagittarius rule the east direction. Taurus, Virgo and Capricorn rule the south direction. Gemini, Libra and Aquarius rule the west direction. Cancer, Scorpio and Pisces rule the north direction. The directions in the prasna (horary) analysis are identified from the placement of the significator planet in a particular sign.

Chapter 5

Significations of Houses

First House: Represents the person, his innate nature and state of health, vitality, longevity, happiness, personality, appearance, prosperity, general disposition in life and the body parts - complexion, head (cranium and forehead) and brain, hair, pituitary glands, etc. For example, weakness of the first house and/or afflictions to the first house or its lord result in a sickly constitution, causing vulnerability to headache, mental tension, paralysis, giddiness, wounds, scars, derangement, brain fever, stupidity, nose bleeding, etc. It causes set backs in professional matters and health of the person. A strong Sun and Mars, as significators for vitality and energy respectively, help as a protective cover in matter of health and status.

Second House: Represents wealth, family, livelihood, nourishment, male child, higher education, food, professional position, spouse, marriage, continuance of married life, possession of precious stones and metals, money in cash, earning capacity, financial status, fortune, prosperity, movable properties, speech, vision and the body parts – face and its organs (nose, throat, mouth, tongue, teeth and eyes, especially the right one), facial bones, upper neck and its bones, gullet, larynx, cerebellum, trachea, cervical region and cervical bones, tonsils, etc. For example, weakness of the second house and/or afflictions to the second house or its lord cause vulnerability to disorders of speech, throat, cervical, gums, eyes, teeth, etc., and diseases mainly arising out of a weak venous system. It also causes problems in professional and relationship matters. It indicates problems to male child. A strong Mercury, as a significator of speech, helps as a protective cover.

Third House: Represents younger brothers or sisters, neighbors, courage, physical strength, sports, initiative, entrepreneurial nature, the power of understanding, leadership traits, short journeys, initiation into spiritual techniques, writing and communicative capability and the body parts - lower neck, shoulders, arms and ears (especially the right ones), hands, shoulders and collar bones, thyroid gland, respiratory and nervous systems, etc. For example, weakness of the third house and/or afflictions to the third house or its lord cause vulnerability to problems of respiratory canal, disorders of thyroid, imbalances in the nervous system, depression resulting in partial paralysis, stammering, shoulder pains, fracture in the collar bone region, partial deafness, respiratory diseases, asthma, tuberculosis, etc. besides bringing setbacks in professional ventures. A strong Mercury, as a significator of communicative capability, helps as a protective cover.

Fourth House: Represents mother, happiness, upbringing, relatives, supporters, basic education, vehicles and conveyances, domestic peace, mind, mental peace, spiritual life, confidence, righteous conduct, comforts, luxuries, country of birth, immovable properties, real estate, land, house, home, assets and the body parts - the rib cage, heart, chest, lungs and breasts. For example, weakness of the fourth house and/or afflictions to the fourth house or its lord cause vulnerability to coronary problems, physical ailments of breast, chest, heart and epigastric region, lungs' disorders, mental disorders, lunacy and the problems connected to the circulatory systems besides causing problems to mother, parents, properties and mental peace. A strong Moon as a significator of mother, Venus as significator of comforts and Mars as significator of immovable properties help as a protective cover.

Fifth House: Represents intelligence, emotions, discernment and discrimination power, talents, memory, creative intelligence, love, speculative gains from investments, organizational ability, success, progeny, knowledge, wisdom, higher learning, training, position, social life, inclinations, spiritual pursuits, disciples and students, devotion, Ishta Devata, mantras, yantras, amulets, resources and merits we bring into life, future, digestion, etc., and the body parts - upper belly, stomach, liver, gall bladder, pancreas, spleen, colon, diaphragm, spine and spinal cord, pregnancy, etc. For example, weakness of the fifth house and/or afflictions to the fifth house or its lord cause vulnerability to diabetes, peptic ulcers, anemia, colic pains, stones in gall bladder, acidity, spinal cord disorders, dyspepsia, diarrhea, pleurisy, etc. besides causing problems in studies and progeny matter. A strong Sun, as significator of digestion - nourishing agent of the body, and significator for learning and job, helps as a protective cover.

Sixth House: Represents disputes, diseases and injuries, debts, enemies, competitors, thieves, fears, doubts, worries, health, sound financial position, maternal uncles, protection against losses through theft, fire and cheating, misunderstandings, confrontation, litigation and the body parts – waist, navel, lower abdomen, kidneys, small intestine, upper part of large intestine, intestinal function, appendix, etc. For example, weakness of the sixth house and/or afflictions to the sixth house or its lord cause vulnerability to problems of appendicitis, poisoning, colics, constipation, hernia, blood urea, psychiatric problems, exhaustion and nervous breakdown besides causing the problems of debts, diseases and disputes. In other words, health, financial position and the position with reference to the opponents is identified through this house. A strong Mercury and Mars, as significators for health, help as a protective cover.

Seventh House: Represents long term relationships, legal ties, spouse, partners in life and partners in business, vitality, potency, fertility, passion, outgoing nature, adultery, moral conduct, pleasures, comforts and life in foreign lands, success in love affairs, conjugal life, home abroad, travel, trade or business, expansion and the body parts – pelvic girdle, lumbar region, bladder, lower part of large intestine, inner sexual organs such as ovaries, uterus, cervix, testicles and prostate gland, etc. For example, weakness of the seventh house and/or afflictions to the seventh house or its lord cause vulnerability to generative organs, venereal diseases, arthritis, gout pains, urination problems, impotency, sterilization, renal problems, etc. besides causing problems in marriage, partnership business and in foreign lands. A strong Venus, as significator for marital relationship, helps as a protective cover.

Eighth House: Represents longevity, research, interest in mystical sciences, occult, inner and outer transformations, past and future events, inheritance, death, will and testament, insurances, easy gains, marital-tie, vulnerability, fear, accidents, obstructions, litigation, bankruptcy, theft, losses, misfortunes, disgrace, disappointments and the body parts – scrotum and anus, outer sexual organs, excretory organs, pelvic bones, etc. For example, weakness of the eighth house and/or afflictions to the eighth house or its lord cause vulnerability to fissure, impotency, piles, boils, chronic diseases, etc. besides causing setbacks to father, husband, self and obsturctions in all aspects of life. A strong Saturn, as significator for longevity, helps as a protective cover.

Ninth House: Represents father, preceptor, spiritual learning, spiritual inclinations, intuition, charity, virtue, duty, destiny on the basis of past lives and resultant happiness, meditation, foreign travel, long journeys of short duration and life in foreign lands, education abroad, grace, luck, general fortune, sudden and unexpected gains, religion, pilgrimages, philosophy, medicine, remedies, past, etc., and the body parts – thighs, left leg, thigh bones, hips, hip joints and the arterial system. For example, weakness of the ninth house and/or afflictions to the ninth house or its lord cause vulnerability to anemia, low productivity of blood, thalassemia, leukemia, high fevers, rheumatism and troubles in hips and thighs, etc. besides causing setbacks to father and fortune. A strong Jupiter, as significator for general fortune, and a strong Sun, as significator for father, help as a protective cover.

Tenth House: Represents profession, career, promotion, livelihood, power, fame, public esteem, status, position, honor, karma in life, character, authority, government, employer, living abroad, ambition, next birth, happiness from male progeny, debts and the body parts - knees and kneecaps, joints and bones. For example, weakness of the tenth house and/or afflictions to the tenth house or its lord cause vulnerability to arthritis, broken knees, inflammation of joints, general weakness, skin diseases and allergies, emaciated body, etc, besides giving setbacks in professional matters and problems to male child. A strong Sun, as significator for organizational capability, helps as a protective cover.

Eleventh House: Represents income, prosperity, gains, profit, friends, elder brother or sister, hopes and aspirations and their fulfillment, etc., and the body parts - shanks, ankles, shin bone, legs, left ear and left arm. For example, weakness of the eleventh house and/or afflictions to the eleventh house or its lord cause vulnerability to circulatory problems, fracture of the lower portion of legs, pain in legs, problems of low productivity of blood, cancer of leg, etc. besides causing problems of income and problems to friends and the sources of support. A strong Saturn, as significator for easy sources of income, helps as a protective cover.

Twelfth House: Represents expenses, losses, expenditures for charity, end of life, exile, life in foreign lands, obstructions in life, separation from family, going astray, withdrawal into retreat, transcendence, enlightenment, seclusion, imprisonment, hospitalization, pleasures of bed, sound sleep and work behind the scenes, as work in a hospital, asylum, prison, military quarters, or monastery, etc., and the body parts - left eye, lymphatic system and feet. For example, weakness of the twelfth house and/or afflictions to the twelfth house or its lord result in problems to the body parts governed by this house, sleep disturbances and weaken the immunization power, etc. besides causing sleep disorder, problems in relationship, problem in foreign land and auto-immune disorders. A strong Moon, as significator for immunization power and mental peace, and a strong Venus, as significator for happy marital relationship and comforts, help as a protective cover.

Fructification of Significations

The signification of the houses fructify under the planetary sub-periods connected with them. The nature and extent of significations are dependent on three things, i.e. (1) the strength of the lord of the house, in case of mooltrikona signs; (2) the strength of the significator of the house; and (3) the influences on the house itself. The significations of the houses containing mooltrikona signs suffer if their lords and significators are weak or they or their lords or significators are under the influence of functional malefic planets. The significations of the houses containing non-mooltrikona signs suffer if (i) they are under close malefic influence (ii) their significators are weak and are under the influence of functional malefic planets.

Extent of Houses

Under the Systems' Approach, we consider one sign per house, so the extent of each house is 30 degrees. The degree rising in the ascendant would be treated as the most effective point. The planets within 5 degree orb of the most effective point, irrespective of the house boundaries, would influence the most effective point as per their functional nature. Irrespective of the longitude of the ascending degree, the functional nature of the planets is identified with reference to the sign rising in the ascendant. The lord of the house will be the planet that rules the mooltrikona sign placed in that house. The results of the planets are analyzed on the basis of placement of the planets in a particular house from the ascendant and, irrespective of their longitudinal difference from the most effective point. The planets placed in a house will be considered in that house only.

Nomenclature of Houses

Angular (Kendra) Houses: The first, fourth, seventh and tenth houses are called angular houses or kendra houses. They mark the angles or quadrants from the ascendant. Planets in angles tend to be stronger and active. Angular houses are similar in character to movable signs. They give power for accomplishment and achievement.

Trines (Trikona) Houses: The fifth and ninth houses are called trines or trikona houses. Strong planets in these houses are important for the intellectual and spiritual achievements. First house is also considered as a trine.

Malefic (Dusthana) Houses: The sixth, eighth and twelfth houses are called malefic houses or Dusthana houses. Planets placed in malefic houses are weak and cause problems.

Benefic Houses: All houses, other than the malefic houses, are treated as benefic or auspicious houses under the Systems' Approach.

Element of Houses: The first, fifth and ninth houses are fiery. The second, sixth and tenth houses are earthy. The third, seventh and eleventh houses are airy houses and the fourth, eighth and twelfth houses are watery.

For further detailed study of each house, the interested readers may study our book, **Systems' Approach for Interpreting Horoscopes**.

Chapter 6

Significations of Planets

The Sun

The Sun is the king in the planetary cabinet. It is the source of light and life. It signifies father, which is the source for bringing into existence and supporting a new born in life. That is why the Sun signifies father and vitality. If the Sun is strong in a nativity, the father and vitality will help the native to grow in a healthy way. The Sun also signifies the king, the master, the government, the president of the country, highly-placed persons, administrators, contractors, chairmen of industrial establishments, physicians, bureaucrats, politicians, police, power, social status and male child. The Sun is secondary significator for husband. As the Sun is personified as a king and doctor, when strong it denotes high administrative positions in government, including politics, doctors in medicine, etc. It blesses with self-confidence, courage, nobility, dignity, ambition, splendor, prestige, faith, loyalty, generosity, authority, power, leadership and creativity.

The Sun is a male planet, hot, dry, constructive, satvic, pitta, and has sturdy bones. Its nature is royal, benevolent and cruel and its temperament is fixed and steady. The Sun gives a square body and majestic appearance. It gives powerful speech. It makes a person courageous and bestows administrative capabilities. Its complexion is blood red and it rules orange, pink and golden colors. It rules the fire element, hot or pungent flavors, the sense of sight, the Sundays, the east direction, copper, gold, ruby, temples, palaces, government buildings, and towers.

The Sun represents head, body, soul, ego, self, intelligence, will power, clarity, self-realization, health, bone structure, constitution, blood, brain, bile, digestive fire, organ of voice, heart as life-centre, right eye for males and left eye in case of females. In case it is weak in a nativity, it gives weak eyesight, headaches, erratic blood circulation, heart trouble, bone fractures, overheating, fevers, baldness, bone cancer, weak immune system, etc. It denotes pride, egotism and self-centeredness. The Sun is significator planet for vitality and life giver in any nativity. It rules the digestive system which provides nourishment to the whole body. The Sun represents the soul. The Sun is also general significator for employment, inheritance, mental inclinations, professional position, comforts, creative intelligence, easy gains, general fortune, higher education, spiritual education and spiritual life.

The Moon

The Moon is the queen in the planetary cabinet. Next to the Sun, the role of the Moon is very important as it signifies mother. The mother brings up the child and is the first preceptor of the child. That is why the Moon signifies mind also. A strong Moon in the birth chart blesses the mother with resources and she is able to bring up the child and develop the child's mental faculties in a peaceful manner. The Moon acts as a nourishing and soothing agent. It rules the senses and the emotions and gives the native the capability of looking after. The Moon signifies the queen, hoteliers, public relations personnel, money-lenders, house-keepers, physicians, nurses, midwifes, healers, psychic abilities, eating establishments, cooks, catering and other professions that deal directly with the people at large. It is secondary significator for wife. The Moon enjoys status in administration by virtue of being the wife of the king. When strong, the native does not have to strive for acquiring status and it denotes affluence, receptivity, sensitivity, imagination, good memory, meritorious deeds and sound habits.

The Moon is a female planet, cold, moist, mild, satvic and its constitution is a mixture of vata (acidity) and kapha (phlegm). Its nature is royal, has auspicious looks, pleasant speech and its temperament is fickle and changeable. The Moon is volatile as it is changing its position daily. Depending upon the brightness of the Moon, while a weak Moon gives a slim body, a full Moon may give a plump body if it is connected with the ascendant or its lord in a powerful way, in isolation. Its complexion is tawny and it rules white and silver colors, the water element, salty flavors, the sense of taste, the Mondays, the northwest direction, bronze, silver, pearl, watery places, public places, hotels, hospitals and ships.

The Moon represents face, mind, consciousness, perception, feelings, tolerance, thought, intellect, receptivity, femininity, sensitivity, imagination, good memory, fertility, general weakness, emotional health and functional health. It governs fluids in body, good quality of blood and glands, tonsils, breasts, lymphatic system, face, lungs and chest. It governs the left eye in the case of males. It governs ovaries, menstrual cycle, uterus, generative organs and right eye in the case of females. In case it is weak in a nativity, besides psychic problems it causes sleep disorders, lethargy, drowsiness, lung problems, mouth problems (including loss of taste), neurological disorders, epilepsy, digestive complains, water retention, blood disorders, anemia, blood-pressure, enlargement of spleen, diseases of the uterus and ovaries, tuberculosis, menstrual disorders, and the native is vulnerable to frequent cough and cold, fever, lack of appetite, general weakness, etc. It denotes hyper-sensitivity, over-reaction, inability to respond and difficulty getting in touch with feelings. The Moon is also general significator for sleep, nourishment, public, social behavior, change, travel, basic education, comforts, emotional peace, family, financial solvency, happy married life, inheritance, income and gains, love and care, mental peace, milk, grains and liquids.

Mars

Mars is the commander-in-chief of the planetary cabinet. It signifies courage both mental and physical. Mars denotes position in military and allied military forces, police, vocations employing fire and metals, engineering, chemicals, surgeons, dentists and executive posts. It governs gangsters, manufacturers, executioners, athletes, builders, designers, entrepreneurs, fire-fighters, martial arts, mechanics and project erectors. Mars is also the general significator of younger brothers, which adds to the strength of the native and becomes a source of strength and courage. The weakness of Mars makes a man lacking in courage and not enjoying the help and comforts from the younger brothers. When strong in the nativity, it denotes thirst for action, passion, ambition, physical strength, goal-directed energy, power to carry through, bravery, heroism, competitive and fighting spirit, vim and vigor.

Mars is a male planet, dry, fiery, tamasic and pitta (bile). Its nature is cruel, unrelenting and active. Its temperament is violent, angry and rash. Mars gives short stature and a stout and well built body, red eyes and thin waist. Its complexion is blood red and it rules bright red colors, the fire element, bitter flavors, the sense of sight, the Tuesdays, the south direction, copper, red coral, places near fire, kitchens, battlefields, places for aggressive and violent or physical contests.

Mars represents bone marrow, blood, bile, forehead, muscular system, nose and external generative organs. When afflicting or itself being weak and/or afflicted it causes inflammations, overheating, wounds, burns, accidents, fractures, skin rashes, ulcers, operations, all sorts of acute complaints, fevers (particularly eruptive), epilepsy, mental aberration, tumors, cancer in the muscular parts of the body when closely conjunct with Rahu, dysentery, typhoid, cholera, pox and boils, etc. It denotes anger, irritability, haste, impatience, inconstancy, lack of drive and courage, and an 'all-or-nothing' attitude. Mars is also general significator for energy, strength, enemy, army, accidents, acute diseases, aggressions, assets, immovable properties, motivation, arguments, quarrels, fights, explosives, weapons, guns, general health, mechanical or technical ability, sports and surgery.

Mercury

Mercury is the prince in the planetary cabinet. It basically rules the rational mind, speech, analytical faculties, sharp intellect, power of discrimination and confidence. Personified as a thinker and knowledgeable in the field of mathematics, Mercury signifies advisory roles, astrologers, financial advisors, strategists, business, commerce, engineering and related fields, research scholars, communicators, editors, authors, accountants, book-keepers, lawyers, experts in analytical works, software engineers, auditors, intellectuals, teachers, etc. When strong in the nativity, it denotes a good communicator with intelligence, rationality, imagination, wit, cleverness, skill, dexterity, verbal and mental ability, shrewdness, sound judgment, humor and flexibility.

Mercury is a eunuch planet, rajasic and tri-dosha i.e. its constitution is a mixture of vata, pitta and kapha. Its nature is friendly and its temperament is volatile and versatile. Mercury has the best appearance, is witty, fond of jokes and laughter, when strong in the natal chart as lord of the ascendant. Attractive features, well proportioned body, large eyes and witticism are its significations. Mercury takes upon itself the qualities of the planets with which it is closely associated. Its complexion is akin to that of grass. It rules green colors, the earth element, mixed or varied flavors, the sense of smell, the Wednesdays, the north direction, brass, emerald, places for business, communication or transportation, airports, post offices, accounting offices, places where public but non-violent games are played, parks, libraries, bookstores and public assemblies.

Mercury represents the lower part of abdomen, skin, mind, nervous system, urinary bladder, bronchial tube, intestines, lungs, tongue, mouth, hands and arms. When weak, it causes psychic diseases, insomnia, nervous breakdown, epilepsy, skin diseases, leucoderma, impotence, loss of memory or speech, vertigo, deafness, asthma, diseases of respiratory canal, disorders of intestines, dyspepsia, etc. It denotes difficulty in thought and communication, timidity, low self-esteem, over-intellectualization and poor discrimination. As Mercury is weak quite frequently, whenever its sub-period is in operation in any nativity it creates tensions in life, lack of confidence, situation of indecisiveness, etc., which ultimately leads to faulty decisions. The effect is more if Mercury is weak in the natal chart as well as in transit at the time of operation of its sub-periods. It makes a person a nervous wreck and can even cause paralysis when closely afflicted by Rahu-Ketu axis, if the ascendant and its lord are also weak or the sign Virgo falls in the ascendant. Mercury is also general significator for communications, eloquence, learning, childhood, logic, maternal uncles, potency, nervous control, respiratory functions, basic and higher education, humor, wit, mathematics, professional position, psychic ability, speculation, short journeys, books, papers and publishing.

Jupiter

Jupiter is a minister in the planetary cabinet. It is the preceptor of the gods. Jupiter is personified as a preceptor, judge and it is linked with the treasury. When strong in the nativity, it signifies the fields of top political and administrative positions, financial advisors, bankers, high administrative positions in government, bureaucrats, lawyers, priests, judges, teachers, astrologers, management experts and administrators. It rules spirituality, services with the state, teaching, law, financial institutions, advisory roles, and is primary significator for husband. If strong, it gives growth, expansion and a humanitarian and spiritual outlook. It denotes wisdom, optimism, faith, generosity, idealism and good powers of judgment. It bestows intelligence and knowledge of scriptures in its main and sub-periods.

Jupiter is a male planet, mild, temperate, warm, satvic and kapha. Its nature is saintly, generous and its temperament is mild, benign and soft-hearted. Jupiter gives impressive and magnificent disposition, thin brown hair, tawny eyes, large body when found strong in a nativity and it rules the ascendant or influences the lord of the ascendant. Jupiter is intelligent and endowed with all the branches of learning. Its complexion is tawny. It rules the yellow colors, the ether (akasha) element, sweet flavors, the sense of hearing, the Thursdays, the northeast direction, gold, yellow topaz, treasuries, banks, vaults, dignified places such as courts of law, prestigious universities, altars, charitable institutions, high level financial institutions, monasteries and missions.

Jupiter represents the hips, the fat tissue, arterial system, liver/ gall bladder, pancreas gland, digestion, absorptive power, hearing power, navel, feet, physical development, palate and throat. When weak, it causes lymphatic and circulatory congestion, thrombosis, anemia, tumors, jaundice and other liver complaints, ear problems, diabetes and other diseases of pancreas glands, etc. It denotes overconfidence, overindulgence and extravagance. The weak Jupiter indicates immorality, greed and materialistic attitude (wanting the best of everything). Jupiter is general significator for elder brothers, husband, male progeny, children, teacher, friends, fortune, justice, education, charity, wealth, creative intelligence, easy gains, general fortune, higher education, income and gains, kindness, mental inclinations, knowledge, happiness, wisdom, morality, virtue, dharma, professional position, prosperity, spiritual education, spiritual life, good behavior, expansion, compassion, optimism, sincerity, honesty, common sense, divine grace and, in fact, all good things in life.

Venus

Venus is a minister in the planetary cabinet. It is the preceptor of demons. Venus is personified as a preceptor and lover. It rules knowledge of life saving drugs and arts. It rules vocations in the field of financial administration, art, cinema, theatres, paintings, music, designing, architecture, interior decorator, modeling, advertising, legal, teaching, hotels, medicines, fashion and luxurious items. It is the general significator for wife and happy married life. When strong in the nativity, it denotes aesthetic sense, worldly knowledge and pursuits, psychic ability, potency, pleasures, correct behavior, luxury, beauty, harmony, creativity, rich tastes, affection, friendliness, love, gentleness, sociability, clarity, charm, harmony, balance, elegance, gracefulness and refined sensuality.

Venus is a female planet, warm, moist, rajasic and its constitution is a mixture of kapha and vata. Its nature is royal, sensual, generous and benevolent. Its temperament is easy going and accommodating. Venus is joyful in spirit, possesses a slim body, is splendorous and has lovely eyes, giving a charming appearance, sharp and beautiful facial cuts, and dark-bright and slightly thick curly hair when found strong in a nativity and rules the ascendant or influences the lord of the ascendant. Its complexion is fair and it rules royal blue and variegated colors, the water element, sour flavors, the sense of taste, the Fridays, the southeast direction, silver, diamond, places of pleasure and amusement, theatres, cinemas, restaurants, bedrooms, art galleries, opera and symphony halls, dance halls, beauty salons, elegant shops and clubs.

Venus represents the pelvis and the sexual organs, desires and yearnings, reproduction, the semen/ovum, private parts, kidneys, face, eyes, neck, throat, chin, cheeks, skin, venous system, etc. When weak, it causes venereal diseases, diseases of urinary or reproductive system, diabetes, stones in bladder or kidneys, cataract, weakness of sexual organs, paralysis, sexual perversions, impotence or inability to have sexual relations, loss of bodily luster, etc., and denotes greed, laziness, vanity, ambiguity, lack of charm, sentimentality, vice and sensual corruption, and lack of taste and refinement.

Venus is also general significator for assets, vehicles, conveyances, comforts, luxuries, art, dance, drama, music, painting, jewelry, romance, family, marital tie, income and gains, prosperity, wealth, materialistic pursuits, opulence, financial solvency, medicine, hypnosis, mantras, ornaments, perfumes, flowers, festivals, professional position, musicians, singers, songwriters, actors, actresses, artists, dancers, designers, engineers, fashion designers, financial advisors, jewelers, perfumers, legal advisors, ministers and teachers. It signifies also people dealing with entertainment, pleasure and beauty as well as people that tend to earn their livelihoods through arts, romance, silver, delicacies, ornaments and finery, poetry, advice or counseling, and fashion design.

Saturn

Saturn is known as ruler of services in the planetary cabinet. It is personified as a statesman and leader of low castes. It signifies jobs requiring hard work with less remuneration, leadership of workers, trying to acquire positions in government services, labor oriented industry, routine workers, engineers, real estate agents, research work, scientists, dealing with labor, stones and mining. When strong in the nativity, it signifies perfection and highest human qualities, spirituality, detachment, concentration, inwardness, dutifulness, reliability, honesty, humility, sincerity, stability, longevity, discipline, responsibility, eye for detail, sobriety, constancy and consistency.

Saturn is a eunuch planet, cold, dry, contracting, short-tempered, worn-out, tamasic and vata. Its nature is cruel, selfish and indolent and its temperament is harsh and hard-hearted. Saturn has an emaciated body, long stature, brown and sunken eyes, protruding teeth, prominent veins, wrinkles, long hands and face, lazy and melancholic nature, coarse and excessive hair when found strong in a nativity and rules the ascendant or influences the lord of the ascendant. Its complexion is dark and it rules black, blackish blue and bright brown colors, the air element, astringent flavors, the sense of touch, the Saturdays, the west direction, iron, steel, lead, blue sapphire, dirty places, slums, basements, mines, inaccessible places, hermitages, retreats, neglected and lonely or melancholy places, abandoned houses and ruins.

Saturn represents the nerve tissue, joints, teeth, knees, shin and part of leg between ankle and knee and secretive system and bones. When weak, it causes constant and painful diseases, all sorts of chronic and degenerative diseases, leg fracture, diseases of glands, skin diseases, paralysis, arthritis, rheumatism, gout, emaciation, rickets, consumption, deformities, coldness of the body, nerve disorders, insanity, numbness, windy diseases and obstruction in the functions of the body, depression, rigidity, loneliness, lack of adaptability, suspicion, slowness, austerity, worry, pessimism, fear, miserliness and selfishness. Saturn is also general significator for longevity, obstacles, suppression, humiliation, fall (from a high position or from a height), poverty, misdeeds, debt, sorrow, grief, form and structure of buildings, coal, wood, steel, denial, delay, elders, labor, land and property, death, disease, misery and sorrows, renunciation, restrictions, subordinates, servants, construction workers, agriculture and agriculturists.

Rahu

Rahu is personified as a diplomat and being a shadowy planet and a legendary master of deception, when disposed beneficially, indicates diplomatic jobs, jobs requiring manipulations with facts, aviators, computer programmers, engineering, flight attendants, highly technical fields, pilots, professions involving juggling, involvement with the masses, involvement with occult or psychic knowledge, dealing in poisons and drugs. It signifies cheats, pleasure seekers, insincere and immoral acts, salesmen, operators in foreign lands, catalysts, wine merchants, drug dealers, conmen, poison dealers, etc. If not afflicting and well disposed, it can give worldly benefits, sudden gains, originality, individuality, independence, insight, inspiration and imagination.

Rahu is a female planet, tamasic and vata in constitution. It is phlegmatic and cruel in nature, eccentric in temperament and gives malignant growth. Rahu creates smoke, has a dark body, resides in forests and engenders fear, giving a smoky and unpleasant appearance due to habits of overeating which result in foul smell and unclean body and nails when it influences the ascendant and/ or the lord of the ascendant. It rules purple and different tones of grey colors, the southwest direction, lead, hessonite anthill, chasms and tunnels.

Rahu is the ascending point where the orbit of the Moon cuts across the ecliptic. It strongly influences other planets. When afflicting, it causes diseases of phlegm, intestines, boils, skin, nervous system, ulcers, worms, high blood pressure, heart trouble, epidemics, psychic disturbances, hallucinations, hysteria, insanity, epilepsy, conditions resulting from all sorts of poisons, alcoholism, mysterious diseases, leprosy, indigestion, gas accumulation in stomach or intestines, insect bite, hiccough, swelling, pain or injury in the feet, cancer, etc. If afflicting or malefically disposed, it generates fears, phobias, nightmares, inertia, dullness, laziness, gambling, confusion, ignorance, escapism, neurosis, psychosis, deception, addiction, compulsive and unconscious behavior, vagueness, illusion, delusion and rough behavior. Rahu is also general significator for transformation, catalysts, immigration and foreign lands or languages, attachment, passion, the one that grasps, paternal grandparents, unexpected events, separation, calamity, reptiles, snakes, snake-bite, toxicity, theft, exile, aviation, deceit, dirt, filth, parasites, imprisonment, insatiable worldly desires, manipulation, drugs and materialistic pursuits.

Ketu

Ketu is personified as a saint and takes a person towards mystic sciences and spiritual pursuits. It takes interest in occultism, spiritual initiation and development, natural healing methods and diets, religion and diversification, services for old and needy persons and rules chemists, pharmacists, priests, researchers and spiritual healers. If not afflicting and benefically disposed, it can give a sudden burst of energy, discretion, liberation, universality, idealism, intuition, psychic ability, compassion, spirituality, impressionability, self-sacrifice, subtleness.

Ketu is a eunuch planet, tamasic and vata in constitution. It is cruel, dry and fiery in nature and explosive in temperament. Ketu gives an emaciated body with prominent veins when it influences the ascendant and/or the lord of the ascendant. It rules brown and fainted colors, lead, cat's eye or chrysoberyl, deserts and forts on hills.

Ketu is the descending point where the orbit of the Moon cuts across the ecliptic. It is strongly influenced by other planets. It is dry and fiery in nature. Its affliction causes wounds, inflammations, fevers, intestinal disorders, aberrations, low blood pressure, deafness, defective speech and gives emaciated body with prominent veins. It is personified as a saint and inclines a person more towards mystic science and spiritual pursuits.

General

The impact of planets decrease or increase depending upon their weakness/affliction or strength and good influences on them in a particular nativity as also due to their placement in a particular house or in a particular sign.

Chapter 7

Planetary Periods

According to their strength in the horoscope, the planets give results of the general and particular significations ruled by them in their sub-periods.

Identifying Results of Main or Sub-Period Lords

Events fructify in the sub-periods of indicative planets. Therefore, it is very important that we understand the method of analysing the dasa (main period) and bhukti (sub-period) results.

Though various types of conditional planetary periods for specific combinations in a nativity are mentioned in classical texts, Vimsottari dasa system has been mentioned for general applications. Based on the longitude of the Moon in the natal charts, the balance of operational Vimsottari dasa is calculated. Thereafter, the planets have their main periods in seriatim. The order of the main periods (dasa) under the Vimsottari dasa system is the dasa of the Sun followed by the Moon, Mars, Rahu, Jupiter, Saturn, Mercury, Ketu and Venus.

The following are the major period of planets under the Vimsottari dasa, which they have in seriatim:

Sun	6 years
Moon	10 years
Mars	7 years
Rahu	18 years
Jupiter	16 years
Saturn	19 years
Mercury	17 years
Ketu	7 years
Venus	20 years

During the major period of each planet all other planets share periods proportionate to their period in the Vimsottari dasa. This share of period is known as sub-period (bhukti) and the first sub-period in any planet's own main period is always its own, followed by other planets in the seriatim mentioned above.

Main Period Lord	Sub-Period Lord	Results
Functional Malefic	Functional Malefic	Will cause suffering
Functional Malefic	Functional Benefic (if strong)	Will bestow good results
Functional Malefic	Functional Benefic (if weak)	Will create only hope that does not get fulfilled
Functional Benefic	Functional Benefic (if strong)	Will bestow very good results
Functional Benefic	Functional Benefic (if weak)	Will bestow average results with misfortune during unfavorable transit influences
Functional Benefic	Functional Malefic	Will cause mild sufferings

Functional Malefic or Functional Benefic	Functional Malefic (if involved in close conjunction or aspect with weak planets)	Will cause grave concerns and/or tragic happenings

If the main period lord is a functional malefic, the sub-periods of the other functional malefic planets cause lot of sufferings while the sub-periods of functional benefic planets bestow good results if they are strong. In the main period of a functional malefic planet, the sub-periods of functional benefic planets create only hopes if these functional benefic planets are weak.

In the main period of the functional benefic planets, the sub-periods of strong functional benefic planets bestow very good results while the sub-periods of weak planets bestow just average results with mishaps during the unfavorable transit influences. During the main period of the functional benefic planets, the sub-periods of functional malefic planets cause mild sufferings. During the main period of the functional benefic planets, the sub-period of functional malefic planets involved in close conjunctions or aspects with weak planets cause grave concerns and/or tragic happenings.

The results of the significations of the sub-period lord depend upon its strength and conjunction(s)/aspect(s) to the same, either in natal chart or in transit. The significations of the house of placement are touched when transit planets create benefic or malefic influences on the sub-period lord. In the sub-period of any planet other than Rahu or Ketu, the following significations are touched:-

1) The general significations of the sub-period lord. For example, the Sun rules father, social status, position with the government, male child, digestive system, heart, blood pressure, etc.

2) The significations of the house where the mooltrikona sign of the sub-period lord is placed. In case some other functional malefic planet influences the most effective point of this mooltrikona house, during the sub-period of the ruling planet

the significations of the mooltrikona house shall not prosper and will face problems indicated by the afflicting planet depending upon its lordship.

3) The significations of the house(s) where the sub-period lord is placed either in the natal chart or in transit.

Similarly, in the sub-periods of Rahu and Ketu their general significations and the significations of their houses of placement as well as the significations of the planets that influence or are influenced by Rahu or Ketu, either in the natal chart or in transit are touched.

Chapter 8

Advanced Analytical Techniques

Salient Features of the Systems' Approach

For the benefit of the readers, the prominent features of the Systems' Approach are being discussed here. Events/indications in life are ruled by the interplay of the planets, houses, signs and planetary periods. The planets during their operating periods bless the person with the significations ruled by them depending upon their strength and placement in a particular horoscope. Identifying the weakness/affliction of planets is not at all a difficult job and can be learnt by beginners or non-astrologers with the help of the techniques given in this book. The Systems' Approach not only increases the accuracy of analysis but also speeds up the analytical process, helps in identifying the results of analysis in an unambiguous manner, consistently and without any confusion.

If the medical personnel learn Vedic Astrology, their dual competence will help humanity at large and will enhance satisfaction and personal eminence of the medical practitioners. Besides the protection from dreaded diseases through preventive astral remedies, the astral remedies tackle the problems of sterility, impotency, help in getting a healthy male child in addition to other areas of life governed by the same planet e.g. professional growth, harmonious married life, acquisition of wealth/property and status. For example, one with defects in the right eye suffers in his professional growth, suffers from loss of status, problems in married life and would be vulnerable to cardiovascular diseases, thyroid glands, etc. At the same time, one with phenomenal ambitions would be vulnerable to nervous breakdown, acidity and runs the risk of a paralytic attack. We hope this gives a clear understanding of the linkage between the planetary strengths and diseases, general problems in life, etc.

The key issues in horoscope analysis are:

(1) Identifying the functional nature of planets in a birth chart;

(2) The techniques for judging the strength of a planet;

(3) The distinction between weak planets and afflicted planets;

(4) The impact of weak and/or afflicted planets;

(5) The orb of longitudinal difference for judging the impact of conjunctions and aspects;

(6) The most malefic influence;

(7) The most effective point of various houses in a horoscope.

Functional Nature of Planets

The functional nature of planets is the key analytical factor in the horoscope analysis. Besides Rahu and Ketu, the planets, whose mooltrikona signs are in malefic houses (sixth, eighth and twelfth) with reference to the ascendant, act as functional malefic planets in a birth chart. For this purpose, under the Systems' Approach the sign Cancer is considered as the mooltrikona sign of the Moon.

For various ascending signs, the functional malefic planets are mentioned hereunder:

Ascendant	Functional Malefic Planets
1. Aries	Mercury, Rahu and Ketu.
2. Taurus	Venus, Jupiter, Mars, Rahu and Ketu.
3. Gemini	Rahu and Ketu.
4. Cancer	Jupiter, Saturn, Rahu and Ketu.
5. Leo	The Moon, Rahu and Ketu.

6. Virgo	Saturn, Mars, the Sun, Rahu and Ketu.
7. Libra	Mercury, Rahu and Ketu.
8. Scorpio	Mars, Venus, Rahu and Ketu.
9. Sagittarius	The Moon, Rahu and Ketu.
10. Capricorn	The Sun, Jupiter, Rahu and Ketu.
11. Aquarius	The Moon, Mercury, Rahu and Ketu.
12. Pisces	The Sun, Venus, Saturn, Rahu and Ketu.

The functional nature of any planet depends on the nature of the mooltrikona house of that planet. It is not related to the strength of the planet. A planet may be weak or strong but the functional nature will remain same as per the defined principle for identifying the functional nature of planets.

Special Impact of Rahu and Ketu

In exceptional cases, when Rahu is well placed in a mooltrikona sign of a planet, without causing any conjunction or close aspect with other houses and planets and its dispositor is strong, Rahu gives good results during its sub-periods for materialistic prosperity. Rahu-Ketu, when exalted, give materialist benefits while debilitated Rahu involves the person in exposed scandals and acute physical sufferings.

The functional malefic planets for various ascendants, mentioned above, may appear to be at variance when seen in the context of the available classical texts, but when you analyze the charts based on the functional malefic planets brought out hereinabove, you would find that all of your confusions disappear at one stroke. The classical principles were laid down by Maharishi Parashara in Dwapara yuga and changes, mutatis mutandis (wherever necessary) have been suggested for the nativities in Kaliyuga.

The functional benefic planets for various ascending signs are as under:

Ascendant	Functional Benefic Planets
1. Aries	The Sun, the Moon, Mars, Jupiter, Venus and Saturn.
2. Taurus	The Sun, the Moon, Mercury and Saturn.
3. Gemini	The Sun, the Moon, Mars, Mercury, Jupiter, Venus and Saturn.
4. Cancer	The Sun, the Moon, Mars, Mercury, and Venus.
5. Leo	The Sun, Mars, Mercury, Jupiter, Venus and Saturn.
6. Virgo	The Moon, Mercury, Jupiter and Venus.
7. Libra	The Sun, the Moon, Mars, Jupiter, Venus and Saturn.
8. Scorpio	The Sun, the Moon, Mercury, Jupiter and Saturn.
9. Sagittarius	The Sun, Mars, Mercury, Jupiter, Venus and Saturn.
10. Capricorn	The Moon, Mars, Mercury, Venus and Saturn.
11. Aquarius	The Sun, Mars, Jupiter, Venus and Saturn.
12. Pisces	The Moon, Mars, Mercury and Jupiter.

Afflicted Planets or Houses

The afflictions to the planets or houses are caused by the close conjunction or aspect of the functional malefic planets in a birth chart. Whenever a planet or a mooltrikona house is already weak for any other reason and is under the close influence of any functional malefic, it is treated as an afflicted planet/house. But when the planet or the mooltrikona house is not weak for other reasons, it can be considered afflicted either under the exact influence of a functional malefic for normal afflictions or under the orb of influence of two degrees for special/multiple afflictions, becoming a weak planet/house for that reason. So whenever any planet or mooltrikona house is afflicted, it becomes weak not being capable of fully protecting/promoting its significations. The significations of the houses having mooltrikona sign of an afflicted planet are harmed more when such planets are already weak for other reasons.

Whenever a non-mooltrikona house is under the close influence of any functional malefic, it is treated as an afflicted house.

If not placed in its own mooltrikona sign, any planet becomes afflicted just by mere placement in any of the dusthanas/malefic houses.

Afflicting Planets

It is very necessary to understand the difference between afflicting planets and afflicted planets.

All planets can become afflicted, but only the functional malefic planets can be afflicting planets.

A transit functional malefic planet will afflict always its natal position by conjunction or aspect, except when placed in its own mooltrikona house in rasi/birth chart. A natal/transit functional malefic planet never afflicts its own mooltrikona house, except when the functional malefic planet is already afflicted and afflicts from a dusthana/malefic house. Dispositor weakness or bad placement affliction is not applicable in this case. The benefit of aspect to the mooltrikona sign of a functional malefic planet is limited to the proportion of the strength of the functional malefic planet.

The Most Effective Point of a House

Besides the natal position of the planets, there is the most effective point (MEP) of each house known by the degree rising in the ascendant. The close impact of the planets in the case of houses is gauged through their closeness to the natal positions. Suppose an ascendant of 16 degrees rises. It means the most effective point of each house would be 16 degrees. In case the lord of a mooltrikona house is weak or in case of non-mooltrikona houses, a functional malefic planet having a longitude between 11 to 21 degrees will afflict these houses either by placement or by aspect. In case the lord of a mooltrikona house is "otherwise" strong, that house will only become afflicted under the single influence of a functional malefic planet having a longitude between 15 to 17 degrees, or under the multiple/special influence of functional malefic planet(s) having longitudes between 14 to 18 degrees. That "otherwise" strong lord will become weak for this reason. The influence of any functional malefic planet over its own mooltrikona house will never be malefic.

Let us see this concept for clarity through an example chart given below. Some of the aspects discussed in this example like conjunctions, aspects, weak planets, strong planets, are explained.

Example Chart 3

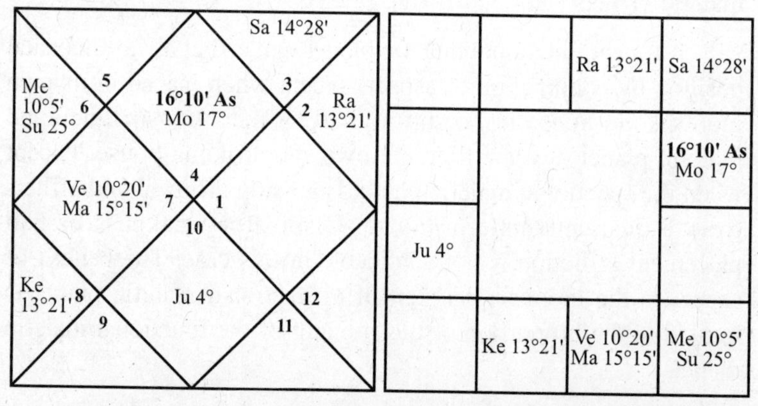

In the above chart the rising degree of the ascendant is 16°10'. This 16°10' becomes the most effective point (MEP) of each house. Now we will see the application of close aspects, close conjunctions, exact conjunctions, exact aspects, single afflictions, special afflictions and multiple afflictions in the above chart.

The Sun is placed in the third house. Therefore, the orb of affliction for the second house by a single functional malefic planet is one degree. There is no functional malefic planet which afflicts the second house within an orb of one degree. Now, the second house can be afflicted by a special affliction or multiple afflictions within an orb of two degrees. We find that the second house MEP is under the special affliction of the most malefic planet, Saturn, from the twelfth house within an orb of two degrees. This affliction not only afflicts the second house, but also make the otherwise strong Sun, weak, due to afflictions to its mooltrikona sign house. Once becoming weak, the second house becomes vulnerable to natal or transit afflictions within an orb of five degrees on either side of the MEP.

The Moon is strongly placed in the ascendant and it forms an exact conjunction with the MEP of the ascendant. It forms an exact aspect to the MEP of the seventh house. The Moon and MEP of the ascendant becomes vulnerable to transit afflictions within an orb of one degree

Mercury is strongly placed in its mooltrikona sign in the third house. There is no natal affliction to the third house and natal Mercury. Natal Mercury and MEP of the third house becomes vulnerable to transit afflictions within an orb of one degree

Jupiter is weak in the chart as (i) it is in its sign of debilitation (ii) its mooltrikona sign is under special affliction of the most malefic planet, Saturn, from the twelfth house; and (iii) it is in the state of infancy. Therefore, both Jupiter and the sixth house are vulnerable to natal and transit afflictions within an orb of five degrees.

The functional benefic planet Mars is strongly placed in the fourth house and it closely and beneficially influences the houses occupied and aspected. Therefore, both Mars and the tenth house are vulnerable to natal or transit afflictions within an orb of one degree.

The functional benefic planet Venus is strongly placed in the fourth house and it beneficially influences the fourth house. Therefore, both Venus and the fourth house are vulnerable to natal or transit afflictions within an orb of one degree.

The most malefic planet Saturn is weak as it is badly placed. It severely afflicts the houses occupied and aspected. Both Saturn and the eighth house are vulnerable to natal or transit affliction within an orb of five degrees on either side.

Rahu and Ketu form close afflictions to the eleventh, fifth, seventh and ninth houses as the orb of afflictions for the non-mooltrikona sign houses is five degrees on either side of the MEP.

Hope this example helps you in understanding the concepts of the most effective point of the house(s), special afflictions and multiple afflictions through close or exact conjunctions / aspects. This will go a long way in your understanding the case studies included in this book and our other books.

The Most Malefic Influence

Mostly, the people seeking advantage of Astrology remember it in the time of distress. Therefore, the first thing is to gauge the strength of the planets so that the influences of functional malefic planets on the weak planets can be analyzed. The most malefic influence in a birth chart is that of the most malefic planet.

Most Malefic Planet

If there is a mooltrikona sign in the eighth house from the ascendant, its lord is called the most malefic planet (MMP). In case there is no mooltrikona sign in the eighth house then the role of the most malefic planet is played by the lord of the twelfth house containing a mooltrikona sign. And if there is no mooltrikona sign in the twelfth house, too, then the role of the most malefic planet is played by Ketu. For various ascendants the most malefic planets are as under:

Ascendant	**Most Malefic Planet**
Aries	Ketu
Taurus	Jupiter
Gemini	Ketu
Cancer	Saturn

Leo	The Moon
Virgo	Mars
Libra	Mercury
Scorpio	Venus
Sagittarius	The Moon
Capricorn	The Sun
Aquarius	Mercury
Pisces	Venus

If the planet or the lord of the house, with which the most malefic planet is forming a close conjunction/aspect, is strong, this most malefic planet creates tension(s) with regard to the matters represented by the house/planet involved. When the afflicted planet is weak, the significations suffer seriously. When the afflicted planet is badly placed, it results in tragic happenings. To understand the difference between tension, serious trouble and tragic happenings consider the situations of fever, jaundice and the loss of a limb ruled by the concerned planet, respectively. Any affliction caused by the triple transit triggering influence of a functional malefic planet can trigger the trouble, especially if it involves a slow moving planet in transit. When the affliction is close to the most effective point of the house, significations of all the houses involved, that is the house occupied and the house(s) aspected, suffer. In the case of the afflicted planets, besides their general significations, the significations of the house where the mooltrikona sign is placed, and the significations of the house where the planet is placed, also suffer.

The Most Benefic Influence

If there is a mooltrikona sign in the fourth house from the ascendant, its lord is called the most benefic planet (MBP). In case there is no mooltrikona sign in the fourth house, then the role of the most benefic planet is played by the lord of the second house containing the mooltrikona sign. In case there is no mooltrikona sign in the second house, then the role of the most benefic planet is played by the lord of the ninth house containing the mooltrikona sign. And if there is no mooltrikona sign in the ninth house, too, then the role of the most benefic planet is played by the lord of the third house containing the mooltrikona sign. For various ascendants the most benefic planets are as under:

Ascendant	Most Benefic Planet
Aries	The Moon
Taurus	The Sun
Gemini	Mercury
Cancer	Venus
Leo	Mercury
Virgo	Jupiter
Libra	Jupiter
Scorpio	Saturn
Sagittarius	The Sun
Capricorn	Mars
Aquarius	Venus
Pisces	Mars

Effective Orb for Judging the Influence of Natal/Transit Conjunctions/Aspects

In the case of influence of functional malefic planets over the most effective points of mooltrikona houses/planets simultaneously strong in rasi and transit, the orb is one degree on either side for normal afflictions and two degrees on either side for special/multiple afflictions, while in the case of mooltrikona houses/planets either weak in rasi or in transit, the orb is five degrees on either side.

In the case of influence of strong functional benefic planets over the most effective points of mooltrikona houses/planets simultaneously strong in rasi and transit, the orb is five degrees on either side, while in the case of mooltrikona houses/planets either weak in rasi or in transit, the orb is one degree on either side. Under the influence of natal/transit functional malefic planets, all planets get malefically influenced.

The maximum influence of the transit or natal conjunction/aspect is when it is within one degree on either side. As soon as the transit influence starts separating, the influence starts tapering down. It is very important to see the strength of the planet on which the transit influence is being studied. For example, if the Sun, being the lord of the fourth house, is placed in the fourth house and its longitude is eleven degrees and is strong, the functional malefic influence of Jupiter, the most malefic planet for the Taurus ascendant, will be effective when Jupiter is between 9 degrees and 13 degrees in the signs Leo, Sagittarius, Aquarius or Aries, while the single functional malefic influence of Mars will be effective when Mars is between 10 degrees and 12 degrees in the signs Leo, Capricorn, Aquarius or Taurus, because the Sun is strong in the natal chart. Please do not forget to consider the transit strength of this Sun. If the Sun in a Taurus birth chart is placed in the sign Libra at a longitude of five degrees then the transit influence of Jupiter over it would be effective whenever Jupiter transits from zero degrees to 10 degrees in Libra, Aquarius, Aries or Gemini, and the transit influence of Mars over it would be effective whenever Mars transits from zero degrees to 10 degrees in Libra, Pisces, Aries or Cancer. However, once the longitude of the transit Jupiter or the transit Mars is 5 degrees, the transit influence would start separating and tapering down but it will clear the affliction only when their longitude is over ten degrees, assuming they are in direct movement. The orb of affliction for a non-mooltrikona house is five degrees on either side of the most effective point. We hope the readers are able to understand this dimension for better analysis.

Measuring Strength of the Houses

In case a mooltrikona sign falls in a house, the strength of the house is gauged through the strength of the lord and the nature of the conjunctions/aspects to the most effective point of the house. In the case of non-mooltrikona signs, the strength of the house is gauged only through the nature of the conjunctions/aspects to its most effective point. You will find in your experience that until and unless there is a close influence of a functional malefic planet on the most effective point of a house, the significations of the house containing a non-mooltrikona sign will not bother the person, at all. That is to say that the person will not seek astral consultation or remedies for the significations of the unafflicted houses containing a non-mooltrikona sign. The rising degree in the ascendant is known as the most effective point of all the houses.

Dispositor

According to the Systems' Approach, the dispositor is a planet in whose mooltrikona sign another planet is located in the natal chart. Suppose in a natal chart the Sun is placed in the sign Libra ruled by Venus. In this case Venus will be the dispositor of the Sun. No planet which is in a non-mooltrikona sign will have a dispositor i.e. the planet(s) in Taurus, Gemini, Scorpio, Capricorn and Pisces have no dispositor. If a planet is posited in Aries, its dispositor would be Mars; if a planet is posited in Cancer, its dispositor would be the Moon; if a planet is posited in Leo, its dispositor would be the Sun; if a planet is posited in Virgo, its dispositor would be Mercury; if a planet is posited in Libra, its dispositor would be Venus; if a planet is posited in Sagittarius, its dispositor would be Jupiter; and if a planet is posited in Aquarius, its dispositor would be Saturn.

When a functional benefic planet becomes dispositor of an affliction, the results of such affliction will surface during the sub period and transit influence of that functional benefic planet.

Similarly, when a functional benefic planet becomes dispositor of a benefic influence or blessing, the results of such benefic influence or blessing will surface during the sub period and transit influence of that functional benefic planet.

When a functional malefic planet becomes dispositor of a benefic influence or blessing, the results of such benefic influence or blessing will also simultaneously surface during the sub period and transit influence of that functional malefic planet provided the functional malefic planet is not involved in a close or exact affliction.

When a functional malefic planet becomes dispositor of an affliction, the results of such affliction will also surface during the sub period and transit influence of that functional malefic planet.

Strong Planets

A strong natal planet protects and promotes its general significations and the significations of its mooltrikona house. Any planet is considered strong when its longitude is within 5 to 25 degrees and it is not in the state of weakness. It can increase its strength if:

a) it occupies own or good navamsa and other divisions.

b) it is under the close influence of functional benefic planets.

c) it occupies its exaltation, mooltrikona sign.

d) it is placed in the Sun-like houses, that is the second, third and ninth houses.

Any planet has capacity to bless the person with its results if its natal strength is at least 60% and it is unafflicted. In such a situation the results may come with some delay and of slightly lower order. With the help of the strengthening measures - gemstones or a Special Power Kavach - the strength of the planets, where it is less than 60%, can be brought to the level of 60% so that it blesses the person with the significations ruled by it.

One can strengthen the weak planets (i) by way of a Kavach if the planetary strength is between 50% to 60%; (ii) by way of a special power Kavach if the planetary strength is between 35% to 50%; and (iii) by way of a special purpose Kavach with gemstones if the planetary strength is lower than 35%.

Weak Planets

A weak natal planet is not capable of fully protecting/ promoting its general significations and the significations of its mooltrikona house during the course of its sub-periods and during the triple transit functional malefic influences. A planet becomes weak when:

1) The most effective point of its mooltrikona sign is afflicted by a functional malefic planet within an orb of one degree.
2) The most effective point of its house of placement is afflicted by a functional malefic planet, within an orb of one degree for mooltrikona signs or within an orb of five degrees for non-mooltrikona signs.
3) It is conjunct or aspected by any functional malefic planet within an orb of one degree.
4) It is combust due to its nearness to the Sun.
5) It occupies malefic houses from the ascendant, except if it is in its own mooltrikona sign.
6) It occupies its sign of debilitation.
7) It is in infancy or old-age.
8) It occupies its debilitated sign in navamsa.
9) It occupies the mooltrikona sign of a weak planet. However, its strength would be equal to the strength of its dispositor.

In case of special or multiple afflictions, the otherwise "strong" planet is considered afflicted (and weak) even when the orb of affliction is of two degrees.

The affliction is special or multiple i.e. when it comes from:

1) a conjunction with/ aspect from the most malefic planet,
2) an aspect from a functional malefic planet placed in a dusthana,
3) a conjunction with Rahu or Ketu (Rahu-Ketu axis),
4) an aspect of a functional malefic planet afflicted by other(s) functional malefic planet,
5) more than one functional malefic planet at the same time,

Fairly strong planet: A planet which has at least 70% power, is unafflicted and well placed, is considered as fairly strong planet.

Mild affliction: An affliction to the extent of 25% or less to a strong or fairly strong planet or the most effective point of a non-mooltrikona sign house is considered as a mild affliction. The quantitative strength analysis for the planets can be obtained with the help of the following insights:

a) A planet will lose strength to the extent of 75% if its mooltrikona sign house is afflicted.

b) A weak planet placed in an afflicted house will lose strength to the extent of 75%.

c) An otherwise strong planet placed in a non mooltrikona sign afflicted house will lose strength to the extent of 50%. Such a planet may give good results in the first place and will cause setbacks later.

d) A closely afflicted weak planet will lose strength to the extent of 75%.

e) A closely afflicted otherwise strong planet will lose strength to the extent of 50%. Such a planet will give good results in the first place and will cause setbacks later.

f) A planet becoming weak due to close combustion will lose strength to the extent of 75% if the Sun is a functional malefic planet. Where the Sun is a functional benefic and it causes combustion to another planet, the planet will become 50% weak for the purpose of transit affliction. A combust planet in its sign of debilitation and placed in a malefic house will have only 10% power.

g) When planets are placed in the malefic houses, they generally lose strength by 50% besides suffering through the significations of the malefic house. The placement in the sixth house can involve the person in disputes, debts and can cause ill health. The placement in the eighth house can cause serious obstructions for the significations ruled by the planet. The placement in the twelfth house can cause expenses and losses for the significations of the planet.

h) When planets are placed in their signs of debilitation, they lose strength by 50%. When planets are placed in their signs of debilitation in birth chart and navamsa, they lose strength by 75%.

i) If in Rasi chart the planet is badly placed and at the same time debilitated in navamsa it would lose strength to the extent of 60%.

j) A badly placed planet in its sign of debilitation will lose its power by 75%.

k) A planet debilitated in navamsa would lose power by 25%.

When the lord of the sixth house is in the ascendant the person gets involved in controversies. Discussing such a person also breeds controversies.

Sun-Like Planets

The second house rules status of the person in the society or with the Government. The third house rules the communication power of the person which is an important aspect for leadership. The ninth house is the house of fortune and rules happiness from father and preceptor. The lords of the second, third and ninth houses, wherever other than the **Sun,** act like the Sun for the various ascendants:

Ascendant	**Sun Like Planets**
1. Aries	Jupiter
2. Taurus	The Moon
3. Gemini	The Moon and Saturn
4. Cancer	Mercury
5. Leo	Mercury, Venus and Mars
6. Virgo	Venus
7. Libra	Jupiter
8. Scorpio	Jupiter and the Moon
9. Sagittarius	Saturn
10. Capricorn	Saturn and Mercury
11. Aquarius	Mars and Venus
12. Pisces	Mars

Any planet placed in the sign Leo has comparatively more power and certainly up by 25% than the actual power of the said planet(s).

When being the lord of the second house a Sun-like planet is placed in Leo sign it gains additional strength.

When the Sun itself is placed in a Sun-like house, it also gains 25% additional strength. In case the Sun is a functional malefic planet when placed in a Sun like house, it should not afflict the house to gain the additional strength.

If the Leo sign is in a malefic house and the Sun is placed in this house, the bad placement of the Sun would not be applicable and the Sun would be strong if not in infancy, old age or debilitated in navamsa.

Let us take an example for understanding the calculation of the strength of the Sun-like planets. Suppose Libra is rising with 22.4 deg. The Sun is placed in the fourth House, close to the MEP and unafflicted. It is not in old age. The MEP of the eleventh house is also unafflicted. This Sun would be strong but not having any additional strength.

Suppose Aries is rising and if Jupiter is in 9th House (Sun-like) in its own mooltrikona sign but in infancy (2.5 deg) and Jupiter is unafflicted, then its strength would be 50% + 25% increase for its being a Sun- like planet which is equal to 62.5%. If Jupiter is placed in another Sun -Like house, its strength will have a further rise of 25%. A planet by being lord of a Sun- like house and by being placed in another Sun -Like house can achieve the strength up to 100% in commensuration to its weakness due to infancy or old age.

In the case of Sun-like planets, the lord of the second house gets the first place, the lord of the third house gets the second place and the lord of the ninth house gets third place in importance.

Significators: In addition to ruling the houses containing their mooltrikona signs, the planets also act as Karakas (significators) for various houses. The various planets act as significators for the houses indicated against each:

Planet	Houses
The Sun	First, second, ninth and tenth houses
The Moon	Fourth house
Mars	Third and tenth houses
Mercury	Sixth and tenth houses
Jupiter	Second, fifth, ninth and eleventh houses
Venus	Fourth, seventh and twelfth houses
Saturn	Ayushkaraka (longevity) i.e. the eighth house

When strong, the various planets act as secondary significators for the following houses/matters:

Planet	House/Matter
The Sun	Fifth house, digestion, heart, leadership, job
The Moon	Tenth house/Public relations
Mars	First house/Energy
	Fourth house/Real estate
	Sixth house/Health
Mercury	Second house/Speech
	Third house/Communication ability
	Sixth house/Health
Jupiter	Ninth house/Spiritual fulfilment
Venus	Twelfth house/Happy married life and comforts
Saturn	Eleventh house/Easy income

Rahu-Like Planets

The mooltrikona sign lords of the eighth and twelfth houses act as Rahu-like planets. The Rahu-like planets give inclinations for greed, over ambitiousness, encroachments, materialistic pursuits, lust, obstructions, mishaps and loss of patience.

Where there is no mooltrikona sign in the sixth house, afflicting Ketu acts as sixth lord being significator for injuries, financial constraints and losses through disputes.

Results of Exchange of Houses or Asterisms

In classical works the situation, in which a planet 'A' is placed in a sign or nakshatra ruled by the planet 'B' and the planet 'B' is placed in a sign or nakshatra ruled by the planet 'A', is considered as exchange of houses or exchange of nakshatra (asterisms). For example, if the Sun is placed in the sign Scorpio and the planet Mars is placed in the sign, Leo, then the classical works consider this as exchange of houses by the Sun and Mars.

Under the Systems' Approach, we do not recognize this concept. Each planet is considered, separately, for its placement, strength, relationship with other planets, etc.

Triple Transit Triggering Influence

The significant events are triggered by the interplay of the relationship between transit planets and natal planets/MEPs. The results generated depend upon the significations ruled by the planets involved, the significations ruled by their mooltrikona houses, the significations ruled by their houses of placement, either natally or in transit, and/or the significations ruled by the natal house(s) whose MEPs are under transit impact. This is called the triple transit triggering influence (TTT) as it is true for the three possible combinations of transit influence i.e. transit over natal, transit over transit, and natal over transit. In other words:

1) Whenever any weak natal planet/MEP is transited by FM(s), it triggers a significant undesirable incident concerning that weak natal planet or that weak house, whichever is the case. This is more so when the weak natal planet or the lord/significator of the weak house is weak in transit too.

2) Whenever any strong natal planet/MEP is transited by FM(s), it triggers a mild unfavorable incident concerning that strong natal planet or that strong house, whichever is the case.

3) Whenever any weak natal FB/MEP is transited by FB(s), it triggers hopes or non-significant happy incidents concerning that planet or house, whichever is the case.

4) Whenever any strong natal FB/MEP is transited by FB(s), it triggers significant happy incidents concerning that planet or house, whichever is the case. This is more so when the planet or the lord/significator of the house is strong in transit too.

5) Whenever planets in transit form close conjunctions amongst themselves, the happenings occur depending upon their

functional nature in connection with the houses with reference to a particular ascendant.

6) If the close conjunction or aspect(s) of planets in transit involve two or more FBs with reference to a particular ascendant, it triggers happy events pertaining to all the planets.

7) If one of the planets involved in close conjunction or aspect in a transit planetary movement is a FM, it harms the significations of the other FB(s) involved with reference to a particular ascendant.

8) If both or all the planets forming close conjunction in transit with reference to a particular ascendant are FMs, it harms the significations of all the planets involved.

9) Whenever any weak transit planet forms close conjunction with or become closely aspected by natal FM(s), it triggers a significant undesirable incident concerning that weak transit planet. This is more so when the planet is weak in rasi too.

10) Whenever any strong transit planet forms close conjunction with or becomes closely aspected by natal FM(s), it triggers a mild unfavorable incident concerning that strong transit planet.

11) Whenever any weak transit FB forms close conjunction with or become closely aspected by natal FB(s), it triggers hopes or non-significant happy incidents pertaining to that weak transit planet.

12) Whenever any strong transit FB forms close conjunction with or become closely aspected by natal FB(s), it triggers significant happy incidents pertaining to that strong transit planet. This is more so when the planet is strong in rasi too.

13) The transit effects are always seen with reference to the natal ascendant.

14) In setting the trends, the sub-period lord has maximum say. However, the transit impacts mentioned above supersede the trend results of the sub-period lord.

15) The malefic transit impact of slow moving FMs like Jupiter, Saturn, Rahu and Ketu is more pronounced when, during the course of their close conjunctions/aspects, they move slower as compared to their normal speed or become stationary. This is true both for natal and transit influences.

16) During the sub-periods of the FBs, the transit impacts of FBs are stronger while transit impacts of FMs are mild. If the sub-period lord is strong, then the transit influences of FBs cause significant happy events.

17) During the sub-periods of FMs, the transit impacts of FBs are mild while the transit impacts of FMs are more severe. If the transit influences are from strong FBs, then the benefic results may be comparatively better but with some delay.

18) The duration of the transit results ceases to exist as soon as the transit close conjunction or aspect separates. The orb of separation as explained earlier would depend upon the strength of the planets on which the transit influences have been created.

19) Whenever a transiting FM transits the MEP of any house, it afflicts that house as well as the aspected house(s). A transit FM never afflicts its own mooltrikona house, except when the functional malefic planet is already afflicted and/or afflicts from a dusthana/malefic house.

20) A transit FM will always afflict its natal position by conjunction or aspect, except when natally placed in its own mooltrikona house.

21) A natal FM will always afflict its transit position by aspect even when transiting its own mooltrikona house.

22) A natal FM will always afflict its transit position by conjunction, except when placed in its own mooltrikona house.

The triple transit triggering influence will help you in understanding the impact of planetary influences more precisely.

For further detailed study the interested readers may study the book, Triple Transit Influence of Planets.

Relative Importance of Planetary Influences

Regarding afflictions, we can have:

1) Afflictions in rasi/natal chart.
2) Afflictions of transit on rasi.
3) Afflictions of transit on transit.
4) Afflictions of rasi on transit.

Afflictions in Rasi, being permanent afflictions, are more serious as they will manifest during all life as malefic tendencies present whenever the sub-periods of related planets are operating. They depend on the strength of the afflicted planets and the number/ proximity/maleficness of the afflictors. In the last three cases, as they are temporary afflictions, their degree of importance depend more on the lack of strength of the afflicted planets, the number/ duration of the afflictions, the proximity/maleficness of the afflictors, and the ruling sub-period in each case. The last one, afflictions of rasi on transit, are even more important than the other two for all the ascendants containing fast moving planets as functional malefic planets i.e. almost all: Aries (Mercury), Taurus (Venus, Mars), Leo (the Moon), Virgo (the Sun, Mars), Libra (Mercury), Scorpio (Venus, Mars), Sagittarius (the Moon), Capricorn (the Sun), Aquarius (the Moon, Mercury) and Pisces (the Sun, Venus, Mars). These fast moving functional malefic planets, that in the previous two conditions are not so problematic, create here serious problems whenever a slow planet in transit comes under their malefic influence. Unless astral remedies are earnestly performed, the problems may come up whenever the planet is weak and afflicted in any of these three transit conditions. The probability increases with the number of the transit conditions involved. The same reasoning applies to the triple transit triggering influences of functional benefic planets.

Regarding how to get the actual strengths of planets for a certain person at a specific time, the different kinds of strengths are:

1) Strengths of planets in rasi/natal chart.
2) Strengths of planets in transit.
3) Strengths of planets in rasi modified by the aspects from transits.
4) Strengths of planets in transit modified by the aspects from rasi.

The strength of planets in rasi is the most important. The last three conditions help and become more pertinent if condition 1) exists. If planets in rasi are weak, they will temporarily become strong only a little by the existence of the last three conditions if no strengthening measures have been used.

Exalted Functional Malefic Planets

Exalted planets if functional malefic planets and at the same time afflicting by close conjunction or aspect other weak planet(s) or the most effective point of the house(s) do cause sufferings with regard to the significations ruled by the said afflicted planet(s) or house(s). The exalted planets, when badly placed, become weak and afflicted.

Role of Planets

A planet plays its role in the following manner:

a) As a natural significator for various things.
b) As a lord of the house containing its mooltrikona sign to protect and promote the significations of that house depending upon its natal strength.
c) Through its relationship with other planetary configurations in a birth chart.

The strength of a planet governs the role of that planet for (a) and (b) above in protecting and promoting its general and particular significations. The functional nature of the planet governs its role as at (c) above.

Analysing Results of Sub-Period Lords

Events fructify in the sub-periods of planets. Therefore, it is very important that we understand the method of analyzing the dasa (main period) and bhukti (sub-period) results. The results of the general significations of the sub-period lord depend upon its strength, placement, conjunction and aspects to the same. The significations of the house of placement are touched when transit planets create benefic or malefic influences on the sub-period lord, depending upon their functional nature whether benefic or malefic. In the sub-period of a planet, the following significations are touched:

1) The general significations of the planet. For example the Sun rules father, social status, position with the government, male child, digestive system, heart, blood pressure, etc.

2) The significations of the house where the mooltrikona sign of the said planet is placed. In case in the mooltrikona house some functional malefic planet is placed close to the most effective point, or some functional malefic planet is closely aspecting the most effective point of the said house, or some planet is closely afflicted then during the sub-periods of the afflicting and afflicted planet(s) the significations of the mooltrikona house shall not prosper and shall face problems indicated by the afflicting planet depending upon its lordship. A natal/transit functional malefic planet never afflicts its own mooltrikona house, except when the functional malefic planet is already afflicted and/or afflicts from a dusthana/malefic house.

3) The significations of the houses where the planet is placed.

4) During the sub-period of a planet all the impacts on the house, which contains the mooltrikona sign of the said planet, also come into force. Due to such influences on the most effective point by a strong functional benefic planet even the sub-period of a weak planet would be blessing the person with good or very good results. Similarly, a close impact of a functional malefic planet on the most effective point of a mooltrikona house may not allow the planet ruling that mooltrikona house to show good results in its sub-periods even if the said planet is strong in the natal chart.

Let us see the application of most malefic planet and most effective point while analyzing the results of sub-periods, with the help of an example.

The 23 degree of Sagittarius rises in the ascendant. Therefore, the most effective point of all the houses will be 23 degree. Any planet conjunct within 5 degrees on either side i.e. within 18 degrees to 28 degrees in any house would be influencing the significations of the house in question in a pronounced manner depending upon the functional nature of that planet. The Moon is placed at 24 degrees in the third house in the sign Aquarius ruled by Saturn. As the

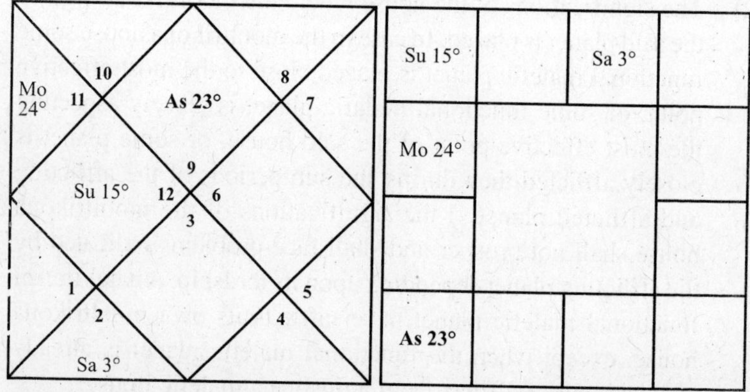

Moon is the most malefic planet, this placement afflicts simultaneously the most effective point of the third and ninth houses, weakening their respective lords and itself. Since the Moon is

conjunct with the most effective point of the third house, it not only destroys the initiatives of the person but during the sub-periods of both the Moon and Saturn it will not allow any ventures/initiatives of the person to succeed. The aspect of the Moon to the most effective point to the ninth house would also cause obstructions to the significations of the ninth house during the sub-periods of both the Sun and the Moon. The Sun is lord of the ninth house while the Moon is aspecting and malefically influencing the ninth house. In such cases if the weak Sun is well placed as in this case, the impact of the influence of the Moon would be a little bit milder than if the Sun is badly placed. As Saturn is very weak due to infancy, bad placement and the exact affliction of the most malefic planet on the most effective point of its mooltrikona house, during the sub-periods of the Moon and Saturn the impact would be quite grave.

Impact of Transit

The impact of transit functional malefic planets is on both the functional malefic planets and the functional benefic planets. The things governed by the planets would be their general and particular significations. Similarly, when the impact is on the most effective point of a house the significations of the house occupied and the house(s) aspected, both mooltrikona and non-mooltrikona houses would be influenced by the transit planet.

Transit of planets over the natal position of functional malefic planets or close aspect of natal functional malefic planets on planets in transit also spoil the significations of the planets in transit.

By transit strength we mean the planet should be strong in transit.

Interaction Between the Sub-Periods and Transit

During the course of the sub-period of a planet the significations of the mooltrikona house ruled by the sub-period lord, the general significations of the planet and the significations of the house where the planet is placed would be touched.

The transit means when the planetary position on any given date subsequent to the date of the birth is studied with reference to the ascendant and the position of the planets in the natal chart.

For example, let us take a chart with the sign Sagittarius rising in the ascendant. In this chart the lord of the eleventh house, Venus, is placed in the twelfth house, ruling losses. During the sub-period of Venus trouble to elder brother, loss of income and trouble to friends is indicated. To cause a death-like event or some serious trouble to the elder brother the transit functional malefic planets Rahu/Ketu may form close conjunction or aspect with any of the three positions:

i) Most effective point of the eleventh house.

ii) Natal position of the sub-period lord, Venus.

iii) Transit position of the sub-period lord, Venus.

The conjunction or aspect of natal Moon, Rahu or Ketu with transit Venus may also cause the same fatality if the natal Venus is weak.

Example Chart 4

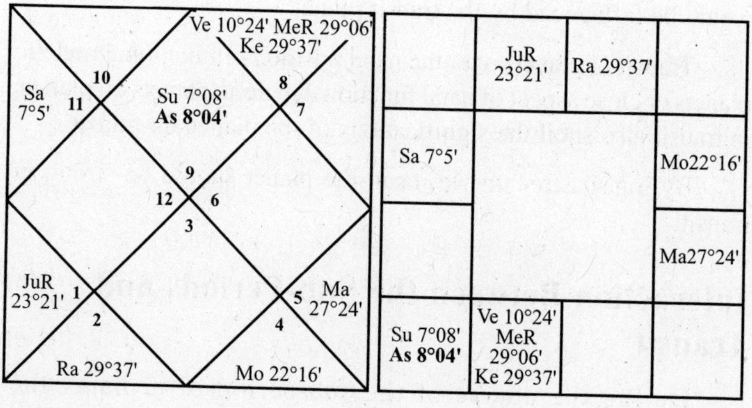

Ve 10°24' MeR 29°06' Ke 29°37'
10
8
Sa 7°5' 11
Su 7°08' **As 8°04'**
7
9
12
6
3
JuR 23°21' 1
5 Ma 27°24'
2
4
Ra 29°37'
Mo 22°16'

	JuR 23°21'	Ra 29°37'	
Sa 7°5'			Mo22°16'
			Ma27°24'
Su 7°08' **As 8°04'**	Ve 10°24' MeR 29°06' Ke 29°37'		

The example chart pertains to a lady born 22nd December 1964, at 0850 hrs at Copenhagen, Denmark 55N41' 12E'35 CE TIME (GMT + 1).

In her case Venus main period (dasa) Venus sub-period (bhukti) started on 30th Oct 1981 and was to run up to 1st March 1985. Now from the horoscope we would see that an incident like loss of an elder brother is seen in the sub-period of Venus as Venus ruling the elder brother is placed in the house of losses. The transit Venus was of 1 degree in the sign Capricorn on 2nd February 1982. It apparently retrograded and came into contact with transit Ketu at 29 degrees in the sign Sagittarius on the 7th February 1982. Up to the 21st February 1982, the transit Venus and transit Ketu were within 3 degrees range. The sub-period lord was not only weak due to its being in infancy but it was also in close conjunction with Ketu. Being placed in the house of losses in the natal chart Ketu is having the inclinations of causing loss with whatever planet it forms close conjunction or aspect with. The person lost her elder brother.

The sub-period lord sets the trend according to its lordship, placement and other natal influences on itself in rasi while the transit/natal planets cause influence whenever they come into contact with the natal/transit position of the sub-period lord.

We hope this gives better understanding into the interaction between the transit results and the sub-period lord results with the help of the above example.

Reliability of Treating a House as Ascendant for Signified Relationship

We cannot treat a house as ascendant for the relation signified by that house. For example, ninth house for father and the seventh house for wife, etc. We can't decipher educational prospects of father, his assets, etc. from the twelfth house which is the fourth house from the ninth house. The status of father in general can be seen from the Sun and the ninth house. The detailed analysis of any relation can only be made from his/her own horoscope. Regarding spouse, children, parents, elder/younger siblings and friends only general indications can be seen from the person's chart. For example, from the person's chart we can see whether the person will derive happiness from his/her children or at a particular time whether the child is enjoying or in trouble but we cannot identify in detail about the educational, professional or emotional matters of a child.

Measuring Capacity of Planets

While studying the impact of a planet, depending upon its strength, during the course of its sub-period both the natal and transit positions of the planet under operation are to be studied.

The result of a particular house will be influenced by a transiting planet when it is near to its most effective point depending upon its functional nature whether benefic or malefic.

A weak planet, too, has the capacity to protect its house if it is well placed, unafflicted, under the beneficial influence of functional benefic planets through close aspect/conjunction or aspects its own mooltrikona house.

Bright Rays

A planet with bright rays means a non-combust planet.

Measuring Strength of Planets in Infancy/Old Age

The results of the planets in infancy or old age vary in degree of strength as per their longitudes as detailed below:

Infancy

When 0 degree power is zero

When 1 degree power is 20%

When 2 degrees power is 40%

When 3 degrees power is 60%

When 4 degrees power is 80%

When 5 degrees power is 100%

Old Age

When 30 degrees power is zero

When 29 degrees power is 20%

When 28 degrees power is 40%

When 27 degrees power is 60%

When 26 degrees power is 80%

When 25 degrees power is 100%

Exaltation sign adds to the strength. The peak point of exaltation or debilitation has very little relevance.

Divisional Charts

The divisional charts are the charts which are drawn by division of houses for specialized analysis of a particular signification; for example navamsa for considering general fortune and marriage, etc., and dasamsa for considering professional aspects in a birth chart. For a detailed study on this subject, you can read the author's book, "How to Study Divisional Charts".

Chalit Chakra

This is a redundant concept so far as the Systems' Approach is concerned. The Systems' Approach identifies the functional nature of the planets on the basis of the ascendant. Each planet is treated in the house in which it is placed. A planet placed in the eighth house going to seventh or ninth house as per chalit chakra can never give good results. Its periods will bestow weak results because of the position of the planet being weak due to its bad placement and there will be obstructions and mishaps. The astrologers, who consider chalit chakra, fail in their predictions.

Evolution of the Soul

The evolution of the soul depends on the strength of the Sun, Jupiter and the lords of the tenth and first houses.

Measuring Afflictions

The quantum of influence of the functional malefic planet (FM) on another planet or most effective point (MEP) of the house is gauged through the closeness of the conjunction or aspect. The afflictions to the planets/houses are caused by the close conjunction or aspect of the FMs in a birth chart. Regarding otherwise "strong" planets and/or MT houses, the normal afflictions are effective within one degree range while the special/multiple afflictions are effective within two degrees range, becoming these otherwise "strong" planets/MT houses weak on this account. The normal afflictions to weak planets/MT houses are fully effective if they are within one degree range while afflictions are 80%, 60%, 40%, 20% and 0% if the afflicting planet is having a 1 deg, 2 deg, 3 deg, 4 deg and 5 deg longitudinal difference, respectively, from the weak planet/MEP of the weak MT house. The special/multiple afflictions to weak planets/MT houses are fully effective if they are within two degrees range while afflictions are 75%, 50%, 25% and 0% if the afflicting planet(s) is having a 2 deg, 3 deg, 4 deg and 5 deg longitudinal difference, respectively, from the weak planet/MEP of the weak MT house. It is most severe if the weak and afflicted planets are badly placed. The experience based on the feedback of the people indicates that these afflictions can be taken care of up to 80 - 90% with the help of the astral remedies i.e. Kavach, gemstones and charities, etc. If the planets/houses are strong, the damage is least. For non-MT houses, the impact of the affliction is 100% to 0% depending upon the longitudinal difference between the FM and MEP of the house as explained above for the weak planets/MT houses. If a planet being lord of a house is weak one should see the strength of the significator (karaka) and the supplementary houses.

Impact of Transit Exalted Rahu and Ketu

The impact of well placed exalted Rahu over the well placed strong functional benefic planets is good for materialistic prosperity. The transit over the weak functional benefic planets gives small gains or creates false hopes. The transit over the functional malefic planets causes anxiety and delays with regard to the significations of the houses where the mooltrikona sign of the functional malefic planet under transit is placed. The impact of the transit of well placed exalted Ketu will be bad only on weak and afflicted planets when Ketu in transit is stationary.

When in dusthana houses the results of exalted Rahu/Ketu are as under:

(a) When in the sixth house, it gives losses through theft and fire, debts, cheating and expenses on treatment of illness. If the lord of the sixth house is strong, Rahu can give some financial gains through manipulations.

(b) When in the eighth house, it can give inheritance, obstructions, manipulating tendencies and increased tendencies for sensual pleasures.

(c) When in the twelfth house, it can give bad health, loss of sleep, craving for excessive gratification of senses, visits to far-off places or foreign lands.

Impact of Combust Planets

When the Sun is a functional benefic planet its conjunction with other well placed functional benefic planets is good and gives exponential growth for the significations of the planets in close conjunction with the Sun. The combust planets suffer under the triple transit influences of functional malefic planets. This can, however, be guarded by application of the strengthening and propitiating astral remedies, to a large extent.

When the Sun is a functional malefic planet or a functional malefic planet or planets are closely and mutually influencing the Sun, the significations of all the planets involved suffer in their sub-periods as also during transit impacts.

For example see the following chart:

Example Chart 5

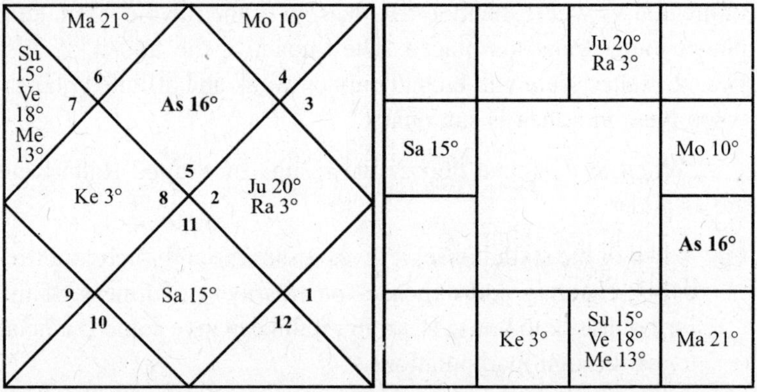

Ma 21° Mo 10°
Su 15° Ve 18° Me 13° 6 4
7 **As 16°** 3
5
Ke 3° 8 2 Ju 20° Ra 3°
11
9 Sa 15° 1
10 12

		Ju 20° Ra 3°	
Sa 15°			Mo 10°
			As 16°
	Ke 3°	Su 15° Ve 18° Me 13°	Ma 21°

All the three planets in the third house are in close conjunction amongst themselves and the conjunction is good except the transit afflictions which will be short-lived if the influencing Rahu and Ketu during the transit do not become stationary. In this chart, the sub-periods of Venus, the Sun and Mercury in the main periods of the functional benefic planets will give good initiatives, increased income and happiness, involvement in writing, artistic pursuits, and status rise through such activities.

Impact of Retrograde Planets in Astrology

The planets are always moving. When we see the record of movement of planets in the zodiac from the ephemeris, we find that the planets move forward. Sometimes, planets appear to be moving back due to the relative position and motion of planets. When a planet instead of moving forward appears to be moving backwards in the zodiac, it is called retrograde. All planets, other than the Sun and the Moon, appear to be moving backward on different occasions. Rahu and Ketu generally seem to move backward.

This is only a visionary phenomenon as this occurs due to different speeds of the planets in relation to the earth. The effects on a natal chart are due to fixed angular position of planets with reference to a particular place on the earth for a particular time, natal or transit.

Though the classical as well as some of the modern commentators have ascribed different views for the results of retrograde planets, the authors are of the firm view that retrograde planets are to be treated in a normal way as per their longitudes, so far as the natal planetary influences are concerned in a horoscope. However, the transit influences of a planet appearing to be in retrograde motion and then direct motion are prolonged on a specified degree(s).

However, for understanding the impact of a transit retrograde planet it is necessary that one learns predictive techniques and methodology for reading the triple transit influences.

Impact of Planetary Combinations (Yoga)

The planetary combinations (yoga) in a horoscope are generated through close conjunctions, close aspects and placements of planets. When two or more functional benefic planets form close relationship among themselves or with the most effective points of benefic houses, they generate good results related to their mooltrikona houses. This type of relationship caused due to the close conjunction/aspect is known as an auspicious yoga. If two functional malefic planets form a close relationship, they cause an inauspicious yoga and destroy the results related to their mooltrikona houses. If one functional benefic planet and one functional malefic planet form a close relationship, this causes an inauspicious yoga that destroys the results of the mooltrikona house ruled by the functional benefic planet. When a functional benefic planet occupies a malefic house, this causes yoga for misfortune related to the significations of its mooltrikona house. Similarly, when a functional malefic planet closely influences the most effective point of a house, it destroys the significations of that house, except if it is its own mooltrikona house.

The impact of Rajyogas and Dhanayogas accrues only if the planets involved are strong. Whenever, the planets ruling benefic houses conjoin or mutually aspect closely, they form good yoga (say Rajyogas) connected with the indications of both the houses involved, provided they are strong. The involvement of a planet ruling the house of income and/or wealth produces a Dhanayoga. In other words, mere location of a planet or a set of planets in a particular sign or house without creating a close relationship through a close conjunction or aspect does not result into any yoga. The planets involved in Rajyogas bless the person with name, fame, wealth, comforts, etc., during their sub-periods.

Similarly, until and unless any functional malefic planet forms a close conjunction or aspect with other planet(s) or house(s) they do not produce any Duryoga or even Kalsarpa yoga. The misnomer Kalsarpa yoga is being propagated by those persons who have failed to correctly identify the functional nature of planets in various nativities and have not been able to pin point the reasons for miseries. Any chart containing the so-called Kalsarpa yoga will not give bad results until and unless Rahu-Ketu or other functional malefic planets cause severe conjunctions or aspects with weak planets or houses in that particular birth chart. Under the Systems' Approach, the analysis is always done with reference to the placement of planets, their strength and weaknesses and their mutual relationship with reference to the ascendant and its most effective point in particular. The planets involved in Duryogas cause miseries/

tragedies as per their nature depending upon their lordships, during their sub-periods.

Another misnomer, 'Neechbhanga Rajyoga' is not coming from the propounding father but has found its place in the subsequent classical commentaries like Phaladipika, etc. The Systems' Approach does not believe in this concept and treats the debilitated planet as a weak planet.

How to Proceed with Analysis for Identifying the Problem Areas

For starting analysis, underline the functional malefic planets. Study the strength of the planets and identify the exact or close conjunctions/aspects. See also if any special/multiple affliction exits. Put a circle around the planets/houses which are afflicted. Now you can start the analysis.

The long-term problem is always with regard to the weak and afflicted planets or the sub-periods of the functional malefic planets in the natal chart. The short-term problem is indicated by the (i) transit of functional malefic(s) over the natal planets, (ii) when transit planets come under the influence of natal functional malefic planets; and (iii) the close afflictions or bad placements of transit planets with reference to a particular ascendant. The good results should be indicated for the significations of the strong functional benefic planets having close benefic conjunctions/aspects.

The position of functional benefic planet(s) in dusthanas or malefic houses make them weak and afflicted but if they aspect the most effective point of the house containing their own mooltrikona sign then despite weakness they are able to protect the significations of their mooltrikona house to some extent. Also, if they are placed in the eighth house near the most effective point of the house then despite weakness it is good as they aspect the most effective point of the second house. In the case of a functional benefic Mars, Jupiter or Saturn posited in the eighth house they also aspect two other houses besides the second house. The detailed study of the functional malefic planets and the planets in malefic houses has been taken up in Chapter 3 of the book, "Predictive Techniques and the Application of Astrological Remedial Measures."

The case studies included here and in all our books bring out the techniques for quickly spotting the prominent events in life. For detailed study of the divisional charts, the readers may refer to our book, "How to Study Divisional Charts".

Insights

Fairly strong planet: A planet which has at lest 70% power, is unafflicted and well placed, is considered as fairly strong planet.

Mild affliction: An affliction to the extent of 25% or less to a strong or fairly strong planet or the most effective point of a non-mooltrikona sign house is considered as a mild affliction.

Whenever Rahu-Ketu axis is placed exactly over the most effective points of houses containing odd signs besides afflicting the houses occupied and aspected, it turns the planets Saturn, the Sun, Venus, Mars and Jupiter weak by afflicting their mooltrikona houses.

Whenever Rahu-Ketu axis is placed exactly over the most effective points of houses containing even signs besides afflicting the houses occupied and aspected, it turns the planets the Moon and Mercury weak by afflicting their mooltrikona houses.

The close influence of the lord of the eighth house or Rahu or the lord of the twelfth house on the lord of the seventh house, and/or the most effective point of the seventh house and/or Venus and the close influence of Rahu on the lord of the eighth house gives indulgence out of marital bond for excessive sensual pleasures and endangers the person with sexually transmitted diseases.

The close affliction of the nodes to weak planets makes one vulnerable to cancerous diseases. Ever since the author, V. K.

Choudhry identified this planetary configuration giving cancerous results in the year 1989, our team had been very particular in watching the horoscopes with such planetary configuration for administering preventive astral remedies and we are very proud to say that in cases where the person had not started suffering from such a fatal disease, the preventive astral remedies proved to be of great help and the persons suspected for cancerous disease did not suffer in the sub-periods of such afflicting/afflicted planets.

A planet placed in the mooltrikona sign cannot exceed the strength of its dispositor.

During the sub period of a planet the results of planets placed in its mooltrikona sign also fructify simultaneously. Prediction of unfavorable results can be/is made for the significations ruled by the weak planets even if there are no afflictions in the natal chart and no planet is badly placed. A strong planet will give beneficial results of its general and particular significations throughout the life. If it is away from the MEP of the house of its placement, it may give results for the significations of the said house in the later part of life. An FM planet does not afflict its own MT sign by conjunction or by aspect. An FM planet will afflict its own MT sign by aspect only if it itself is afflicted by another FM planet. Dispositor weakness or bad placement affliction is not applicable in this case. The benefit of aspect to the MT sign of FM is limited to the proportion of the strength of the FM.

The third house also rules learning, comprehension, vitality, leadership, vision and success.

The placement of the tenth lord in the second house gives professional education.

The strength of Sun or the Sun like houses or planets improve the results of other planets to some extent.

In Divisional Charts we see the influence of FMs of DCs. The strong affliction of MMP to the significators of longevity, the placement of planets in the 8th house and the afflicted Moon cause short life span.

Close afflictions to MEP of the houses harm the main significations of the house.

The strong planets give results without much efforts while the weak planets need more efforts with little/delayed success. Give due consideration to placement of the planets. The planets placed in the third house take the person to MBA / marketing like studies. The strong planets bring brilliance coupled with stability. The weak planets show their impact through instability.

The affliction depends upon the closeness of the functional malefic planet to the planet/house which is being afflicted.

The afflicting power of the functional malefic planet does not reduce due to its weakness. The afflicting power of the functional malefic planet increases when it is placed in a malefic house or it itself is under affliction.

If the planet/house under affliction is weak, the impact of affliction will be more.

For strong planet the orb of affliction is one degree.

The orb of affliction is two degrees for strong planets in the following cases:

- multiple affliction;
- affliction by the most malefic planet;
- affliction by Rahu and Ketu both;
- affliction from a planet placed in dusthana (malefic house),

For weak planets/houses the orb of affliction is five degrees.

The affliction to the MEP of houses is more severe in comparison to the affliction to a planet.

The karma results arise through the principles of divine justice. Jyotish/Astral remedies are the means for alleviating the karma results.

The important tools for predictive accuracy are the functional nature of planets, strength of planets, inter-relationships of planets, divisional charts, impact of Rahu & Ketu, planetary periods and triple transit triggers.

For differentiating between

- having issues in a particular area throughout life
- enjoying good results in a particular area but in some sub-periods facing issues and drawbacks

The guiding principles are that the planets give results as per their strength in their sub periods. Transit influences take precedence over sub period results. The strong/exact afflictions to natal planets are not easy things to be dealt with. The continuous propitiation with strengthening of afflicted planets help. Some other strong planets in the birth chart help in bringing down the impact of strong afflictions. The strong planets, in general, give good results for their significations throughout the life. Where there are no strong or well placed planets, there is limited hope of things turning good. To answer questions for timing of events, see the natal and transit planetary strengths, operating sub period and transit to answer these questions. For example, in a query for job, if the natal determinants of profession and the Sun are strong or well placed with at least 60% power and there is no transit affliction the person is likely to get work in a couple of months' time. Another month or so can be added if Rahu-Ketu are stationary. For rest of the people it may take longer time and they need strengthening of their planets and propitiation of the planets causing afflictions.

Whenever there are double or multiple close/exact afflictions, these take first priority in giving their results. In case such close/ exact afflictions of MMP and Rahu-Ketu axis are suffered by the prime significator of the marriage, the marriage can be delayed inordinately or even denied. In such cases the use of a special purpose Kavach and continuous special propitiatory remedies become absolutely essential.

Decade per degree rule: The impact of conjunctions and aspects is measured in terms of a decade per degree of closeness. If it is an exact aspect or conjunction between the two planets the impact is felt in the sub periods falling in the first ten years of life. If there is a close aspect or conjunction with a longitudinal difference of one to two degrees the impact is felt in the sub periods of the planets falling in the second decade. If there is a close aspect or conjunction with a longitudinal difference of two to three degrees the impact is felt in the sub periods of the planets falling in the third decade. If there is a close aspect or conjunction with a longitudinal difference of three to four degrees the impact is felt in the sub periods of the planets falling in the fourth decade. If there is a close aspect or conjunction with a longitudinal difference of four to five degrees the impact is felt in the sub periods of the planets falling in the fifth decade.

The results can be further influenced by stationary transit influence or the strength of the planets involved.

When any exalted functional malefic planet, other than Mercury, is conjunct with the MEP of the house of its placement, it becomes weak.

Strong Venus hastens marriage.

Strong Sun brings down the level of sufferings due to afflictions.

Metals ruled by planets: The Sun rules copper and gold. The Moon rules silver. Mars rules copper. Mercury rules brass. Jupiter rules gold. Venus rules silver and aluminum. Saturn rules iron, minerals and crude.

Planetary castes and Nature: Those with strong influence of Jupiter go in the learning, teaching, training, development and spiritual work - Brahmins. Those with strong Sun and Mars go for administrative / organisation profession, government assignments & security forces are fighters - Kshatriyas. Those with strong Moon, Mercury and Venus go for trading / business ventures - vaishayas. Those with weak planets and strong influences of Saturn and Rahu go for routine jobs – Sudra.

While afflicting, the mooltrikona sign lords of the eighth and twelfth houses act as Rahu like planets.

The balance sheet of past lives is in the form of the birth chart. Purva punyas (good deeds of past lives) are seen from the IX house. Karma of this life (deeds of this life) are seen through the fifth and tenth houses. The strong planets represent the good Karma from past lives, while the weak planets and afflictions to planets and houses represent the bad karma brought forward. Afflictions point to very bad Karma, whereas weaknesses represent milder bad karma.

Vedic Astrology is an ancient universal knowledge on which we offer our views as other authors/astrologers have done in the past and are doing in the present.

The items for propitiation suggested are based on the planetary tastes mentioned in the vedic literature and bhoota yagyam - one of the five great sacrifices. These have nothing to do with the remedies suggested in other books.

While we have expressed our views based on our experience, the readers are free for their own views and beliefs and for adopting the Systems' Approach brought out by us for interpreting the horoscopes.

The problems and mishaps are represented by the weak and weak and/or afflicted planets.

When the natal Moon is afflicted by Rahu, Rahu-like planets or is placed in the Rahu-like houses the person becomes more sensitive and especially to unfavorable incidents.

The exact affliction to badly placed lord of fourth or second or ninth or third house lord (most benefic planet) reduces the strength of other strong planets in the natal chart.

The weakness of the lord of the eighth house makes the father vulnerable to damage, both in terms of longevity and in terms of finances.

The weakness of the lord of the eighth house or fourth house curtails the financial resources or longevity of father. In Pisces ascendant there is no MT sign in the ninth and fourth houses. So, the eighth house becomes pertinent significator of the longevity of the father. We also consider the strength of the Sun in the natal chart as it is significator for father.

Affliction to the ascendant in any divisional chart by the eighth lord of the divisional chart is equally serious as the affliction to the prime determinants placed in eighth house of the divisional chart.

In divisional charts besides the affliction of R&K, the afflictions by the functional malefic planets of the divisional charts should be considered and the afflictions by the functional malefic planets of natal chart are not considered. Bad placements are also considered in the divisional charts.

The close influence of Rahu on the third lord makes the person adventurous.

The exact / close aspect of Rahu makes the person greedy and does not allow him/her to feel contented.

Suppose there is an exact conjunction/aspect of planets in the birth chart or there is an exact conjunction/aspect of a planet with the most effective point of a house in the birth chart. When this position of exact conjunction or aspect develops prolonged malefic transit influence the person faces multiple challenges in his/her life simultaneously.

The placement of planets is an important factor in horoscope reading. The placement of a planet gives results connected with the significations of the house ruled by the planet with the house of placement despite its weakness or despite the planet being away from the most effective point of the house. If a functional malefic planet is on the most effective point of a house it causes problems but the problems may be connected with the significations ruled by the said planet. For example, if the lord of the second is placed in the twelfth house, the person may move to a distant place or a foreign land in connection with the professional status. If the second lord is placed in the tenth house the person may acquire status in life due to his/her professional achievements. If the second lord is placed in the fifth house, one may acquire professional qualification and acquire status through the same. If the second lord is placed in the seventh house one may attain status in a foreign land. If the second lord is placed in the fourth house one may attain status by being born in a resourceful family. If the second lord is placed in the eighth house one may attain status in life with some delay. If the second lord is placed in the ninth house one may be lucky to attain the status in life without much efforts with the help of parents and preceptor. If the second lord is placed in the eleventh house, one may acquire status in life because of good earnings in life and because of friendship with highly placed persons. If the second lord is placed in the second house, one may enjoy good status in life due to the appointment with the state or due to the family status. If the second lord is placed in the ascendant one may enjoy authoritative status. The placement of the Sun and Mars in the third house brings courage. The close influence of the fifth lord on the tenth house brings the element of intellect. The placement of the planets in the second house, which rules status, brings status as per significations ruled by them. The good placement of eighth lord in the house of status brings easy gains with small or little efforts. The planets in the first house influence the personality traits. The planets in the second house contribute to professional ventures. The planets in the third house bring entrepreneurial ventures and opportunities. The planets in the fourth house contribute to assets. The planets in the fifth house contribute to learning. The planets in the sixth house involve the person in debts, health problems and conflicts. The planets placed in the seventh house give rise to living in foreign lands, long journeys and associations. The planets placed in the eighth house cause easy gains, obstructions and delays. The planets placed in the ninth house involve the person in family or religious traditions or spiritual pursuits. The planets placed in the tenth house involve the person in professions connected with the planet. The planets placed in the eleventh house contribute to earnings through the significations ruled by the concerned planets. The planets placed in the twelfth house take one to distant places and foreign lands and can cause losses and expenses.

During the sub period of Mercury things work with stresses and strains even when Mercury is strong and or well placed in the natal chart. This is due to the volatile strength of Mercury in transit. When Mercury is weak in the natal chart the results in its sub period do create stresses and strains. The situation becomes further difficult when either of the Sun or Mercury is a functional malefic planet.

Whenever the lord of the twelfth house is placed in the sixth house or afflicts some planet from the sixth house closely, there are chances of problems with governement which may result in arrest, legal penalties, imprisonment, etc.

Eclipses:

Eclipses, in general, does not make a strong or prolonged impact for living persons until and unless some slow moving planet is stationary or moving utterly slow or appearing retrograde near the degree of some natal planet in the chart of an individual or nation.

For those who are taking birth, there are chances that there are strong close afflictions to the Sun and/or the Moon or any other planet in the natal chart. This can certainly cause prolonged problems for the person.

SA is an all pervasive framework, touching upon all aspects of predictive astrology - both natal and mundane.

Caution: Astrologers do not have a television set and cannot give running commentary. The best thing is in the shortest possible time, indicate the strong and weak areas in chart and prescribe appropriate astral remedies. One acquires credentials or good reputation as an astrologer with one's competence over a period of time.

Chapter 9

How to Draw a Horoscope

Methodology for Finding Ascendant and Planetary Longitudes

The preparation of a horoscope involves working out of ascendant, planetary longitudes, balance of dasa, drawing rasi, navamsa and other divisional charts. We shall take up these, one by one, for a birth which took place at 0315 hours (3.15 AM) at Delhi on 6th September, 1991. Those who have access to internet can buy the Jyotish tools software from the website www.Jyotishtools.com. However, we are explaining the methodology to work out a horoscope for those who do not have access to Internet.

How to Find Out the Ascendant

For this we require a book, "**Tables of Ascendants**" by Shri N. C. Lahiri. Though the use of tables has been illustrated in the beginning of the said book, yet we would work out the ascendant for our example horoscope.

First of all, we shall note down the following particulars for the place of birth (Delhi) from the Table of Principal Cities appended to the book:

(i) Latitude 28° 39' North

(ii) Longitude 77° 13' East

(iii) Local time correction

LMT from IST (-)21 minutes 8 seconds

(iv) Correction to Indian Standard Time + 03 seconds

The calculations are done in 2 stages.

First Stage

We proceed with the first stage to find out the corrected time interval.

	h	m	s
Time of birth	3 -	15 -	00 AM
Apply local time correction	(-) 0 -	21 -	08
Local mean time	2 -	53 -	52
As the LMT is before Noon	(-) 12 -	00 -	00
We shall find out how much time is left for noon of 6-9-1991 (In case the time is after Noon i.e., recorded in PM, 1200 hours need not be deducted from LMT)	(-) 9 -	6 -	8
Time interval increased by 10 second per hour (Table IV in the book)	(-) 0 -	1 -	31
Corrected Time Interval	(-) 9 -	7 -	39

Second Stage

In this stage we find out the sidereal time (ST) for the epoch.

Sidereal time for 6th Sept, 1900 (Ref Table I)	10 -	59 -	34
Correction for the year 1991 (Ref Table II)	(-)		10
	10 -	59 -	24
Apply correction to IST as noted by us earlier	+		03
Therefore ST same date Noon of the place	10 -	59 -	27

Now we have to merge the two calculations. We will work out the ST for the epoch

	h	m	s
ST at Noon	10 -	59 -	27
Corrected time interval (Before Noon)	(-) 9 -	7 -	39
ST for the epoch	1 -	51 -	48

Note: If the corrected time interval is after Noon the same will be added to ST at Noon to find out ST for the epoch.

Now we will find out the Ascendant with the ST for the epoch obtained. As the latitude of the place is 28° 39' North, we shall use the table for this latitude from the book.

	S	o	'
For ST 1 hour and 48 minutes asdt is	3 -	12 -	26
Proportionate variation for 3 minutes & 48 seconds the Asdt is	0 -	00 -	48
Therefore for ST 1 hour 51 minutes & 48 seconds the Asdt is	3 -	13 -	14
Ayanamsa correction for 1991 obtained from Table for Ayanamsa correction given in the book	(-)		44
Ascendant	3 -	12 -	30

This is read as Cancer12° 30' as 3 signs have already passed and the Cancer Ascendant is in progress. The 12° 30' will be treated as the most effective point (MEP) of all the houses in our illustration.

How to Find Out Planetary Position

For finding out the planetary position, we shall make use of condensed ephemeris by Mr. N. C. Lahiri which are used by most of the astrologers for the sake of reliability.

The condensed ephemeris is available right from 1900 onwards. Before making use of the ephemeris, we shall first find out for what time the position of planets has been given. In the ephemeris for the year 1900 to 1941, the planetary position has been given for 5:30 PM and thereafter for all years the planetary position has been given for 5:30 AM. The position of the Moon has been given for each day in all the year-wise ephemeris. The position of other planets has been given on weekly basis in the case of years 1900 to 1941, on alternate day basis for the years 1941 to 1995 and daily basis for the years 1996 and onwards. The position of Rahu has been given as on 1st of every month, at the end of the position of planets.

After carefully considering one's requirement one may proceed for finding out the planetary longitudes for the given time. For our example we find that position of planets on daily basis at 5:30 AM is available. We can proceed to find out the position of planets as given in the table on the next page.

As you have seen in the table on the next page we have, with the simple method of proportion, obtained longitudes for the requisite time. As you have observed the planetary longitudes of Venus, Saturn and Rahu were less on 6-9-1991 in comparison to 5-9-1991 and this indicates the apparent retrograde motion of the planets. While noting down the longitudes of the planets, we use "(R)" with longitudes of planets indicating apparent retrograde motion.

We note down the longitudes of Ascendant and planets as under:

	s	-	o	-	'
Ascendant	3	-	12	-	30
Sun	4	-	19	-	05
Moon	3	-	14	-	29
Mars	5	-	09	-	14
Mercury	4	-	01	-	17
Jupiter	4	-	04	-	54
Venus	3	-	28	-	22 (R)
Saturn	9	-	7	-	08 (R)
Rahu	8	-	23	-	52
Ketu	2	-	23	-	52

Ketu is always 180° apart from Rahu in Rasi (birth) chart i.e. in the seventh house from Rahu and having identical degrees as that of Rahu.

Planets	Sun	Moon	Mer	Ven	Mars	Jup	Sat	Rahu
	s ° '	s ° '	s ° '	s ° '	s ° '	s ° '	s ° '	s ° '
Position as at 5:30 AM on 6/9/91	04-19-10	03-15-51	04-01-21	03-28-20	05-09-18	04-04-55	09-07-08	08-23-52
Position as at 5:30 AM on 5/9/91	04-18-12	03-01-16	04-00-40	03-28-39	05-08-39	04-04-42	09-07-10	08-23-54
Difference	58	14-35	41	(-) 19	39	13	(-) 02	(-) 02
Movement of Planets during 24 hours	58	14-35	41	(-) 19	39	13	(-) 02	(-) 02
Proportionate difference for 2 hours and 15 minutes	5	1-22	4	(-) 02	4	1	(-) 00	(-) 00

	Sun	**Moon**	**Mer**	**Ven**	**Mars**	**Jup**	**Sat**	**Rahu**
Planetary longitudes for 6/9/91, 5:30 AM	04-19-10	03-15-51	04-01-21	03-28-20	05-09-18	04-04-55	09-07-08	08-23-52
Less difference for 2 hours & 15 minutes	(-) 5	(-) 1-22	(-) 4	(+) 2	(-) 4	(+) 01	0	0
Planetary longitudes for 6/9/91, 3:15 AM	04-19-05	03-14-29	04-01-17	03-28-22 (R)	05-09-14	04-04-54	09-07-08 (R)	08-23-52

How to find out the Balance Main Period (Dasa) at Birth

See in which nakshatra the longitude of the Moon falls. In this case it falls in Pushya or we can say the Moon is in Pushya nakshatra. The Pushya nakshatra is ruled by Saturn and therefore, at birth, dasa of Saturn will be in progress. How much dasa (main period) of Saturn is left is found out in two ways. Firstly through the table "Balance of Vimshottari Dasa" by Longitude of the Moon given at the end of all ephemeris. Secondly by method of proportion. The extent of a nakshatra is 13° 20' or 800'. Therefore in 800 minutes of longitude of nakshatra, the main period of different planets take its course in full e.g. the Sun's main period of 6 years is of 2191.5 days (6 x 365.25).

In our example case, the Moon is in Pushya Nakshatra. The longitude of Pushya Nakshatra is from 3^{s}-3°-20' to 3^{s}-16°-40' and the Moon's longitude is 3^{s}-14°-29'. Therefore, the Moon has still to cover 2°-11' to reach the end of longitude of Pushya Nakshatra. The balance of Saturn dasa at birth would be proportionate to the longitude yet to be covered by the Moon i.e. 2°-11' in Pushya Nakshatra.

End of Pushya Nakshatra		3s	-	16°	-	40'
Moon's longitude	(-)	3s	-	14°	-	29'
Longitude to be covered by the Moon to reach the end of longitude of Pushya Nakshatra				2°	-	11'
Saturn's total dasa in 800'						19 years (19 x 365.25) or 6939.75
Saturn's balance dasa proportionate to 2°-11'-(131'-)						6939.75 x 131' / 800' = 1136.38 days =3 years 1 month 11 days

In the native's life, the main period of Saturn will operate upto 16th October 1994 (6-9-91+3 years, 1 month and 10 days) and thereafter the main period of Mercury will start.

Drawing the Rasi (Birth) and other charts

For drawing Rasi chart as per longitudes earlier noted, first of all put sign 4 in the first house (Asdt) and then put signs in seriatim in all the houses as under:

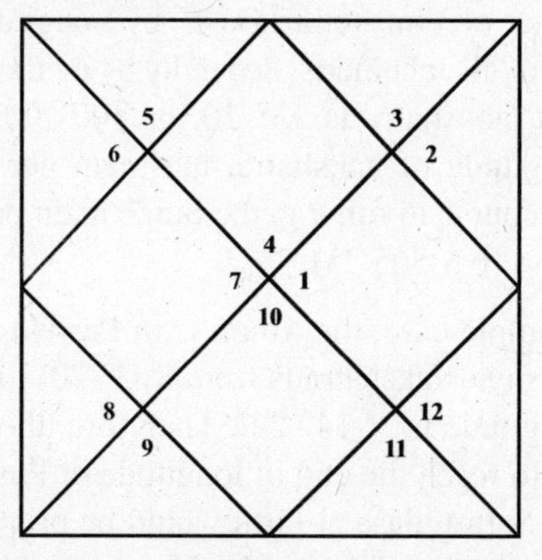

Now place various planets in the chart on the basis of longitudes worked out as under:

Me 1°16' Ju 4°54'
Su 19°05'
Ke 23°53'
5
Ma 9°14' 6
As 12°30'
Mo 14°28'
VeR 28°22'
3
2
4
7
1
10
8
SaR 7°08'
12
9
11
Ra 23°53'

			Ke 23°53'
			As 12°30' Mo 14°28' VeR 28°22'
SaR 7°08'			Me 1°16' Ju 4°54' Su 19°05'
Ra 23°53'			Ma 9°14'

(Note: Minor difference in the longitudes of the Moon, Mercury, Rahu and Ketu are due to the computerised calculations.)

Thereafter, with the help of tables given for preparation of navamsa chart at the end of the book, we shall prepare navamsa chart, which will be as under:

Mo Ra
Su
8
6
9
As
5
7
10
4
1
11
Me
3
12
2
Ma Ve
Sa
Ju Ke

Ma Ve Sa	Me	Ju Ke	
	Mo Ra	**As**	Su

Similarly, we can make other divisional charts as per requirement.

Dasamsa chart will be as under:

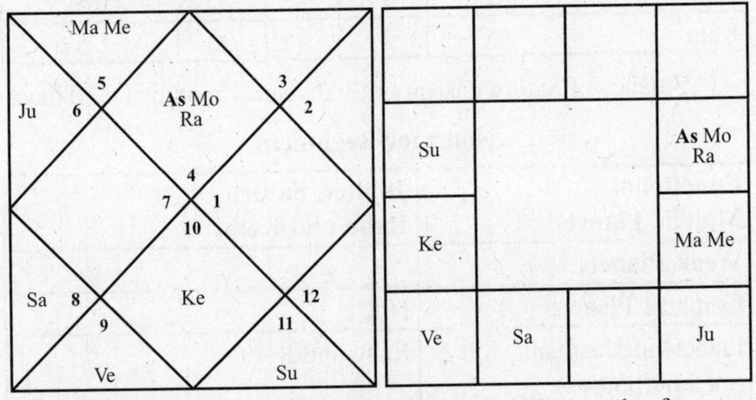

The chart, fully prepared can be recorded as under for easy comprehension with notes for beginners.

Name XYZ

Date of Birth 6th Sept., 1991

Place of Birth Delhi Latitude 28° 39' N
Longitude 77° 13' E

Time of Birth 03.15 AM

	s	-	o	-	'
Ascendant	3	-	12	-	30
Sun	4	-	19	-	05
Moon	3	-	14	-	29
Mars	5	-	09	-	14
Mercury	4	-	01	-	17
Jupiter	4	-	04	-	54
Venus	3	-	28	-	22 (R)
Saturn	9	-	7	-	08 (R)
Rahu	8	-	23	-	52
Ketu	2	-	23	-	52

Balance of Saturn dasa at birth: 3 years 1 month and 10 days.

Notes for Beginners

Functional Malefic Planets	**Jupiter, Saturn Rahu and Ketu**
Weak Planets	
Combust Planets	NIL
Planets in Dusthana (malefic houses)	Rahu and Ketu
Debilitated Planets	NIL
Planets in Infancy	Mercury, Jupiter is in mild infancy
Planets in Old Age	Venus
Planets Debilitated in Navamsa	The Moon, Rahu and Ketu

Afflicted Planets

Functional Malefic planets are not in close conjunction/aspect with any planet and MEP of the houses except Jupiter's close conjunction with Mercury.

Planets Influencing MEP of Houses

The Moon influences the MEPs of the ascendant and the seventh house.

Mars influences the MEPs of third, sixth, ninth and tenth houses.

Note: While you can practice the casting of charts, you can proceed with learning and using predictive techniques with the help of computer-made horoscopes. Lack of mastery in casting a horoscope is not a handicap for pursuing study of predictive techniques.

The planetary influences in a horoscope are studied through the natal (birth chart) conjunctions, aspects and placements. The conjunctions and aspects help us in identifying the auspicious and inauspicious planetary configurations. The placement of a planet in a particular horoscope links the significations of the house containing mooltrikona sign of the said planet with the significations of the house of its locations. A planet placed in malefic house indicates suffering of the significations ruled by the said planet in the birth chart. While discussing the case studies the term, 'the lord of a particular house' refers to the house where the mooltrikona sign of the said planet is placed.

For identifying the afflicting close conjunctions/aspects, first of all underline the functional malefic planets. Then identify the close conjunctions/aspects and encircle the planets under the close influence of the functional malefic planets.

Chapter 10

Fundamentals for Studying a Horoscope

Before proceeding with discussion on the integrated analytical technique known as Systems' Approach for interpreting horoscopes, let us bring out the methodology for a quick overall view of the horoscope.

As a golden principle to avoid disgrace to the science and the astrologers, no attempt for prediction should be made until and unless the horoscope has been cast properly, the planetary strengths have been identified and the operating planetary periods and sub-periods have been worked out.

The predictions made by astrologers well versed in (i) identifying right functional nature of the planets in the birth chart, (ii) identifying the planetary strengths (iii) identifying the placements of planets (iv) identifying relationships developed through close conjunctions / aspects, (v) identifying the triple transit influences (vi) predictive techniques brought in previous chapters of the book (vii) proper analysis of sub period results and (viii) with appropriate astrological remedies advice have better chance of coming true.

Prime Factors:

First of all, the position of the lord of ascendant and the ascendant is to be seen as the whole activity revolves around the ascendant. The lord of the ascendant would be applicable only to those ascendants which contain mooltrikona sign of a planet. In all cases we have to see the influences of the various planets on the first house either by placement or conjunction/aspect over its most effective point. All the results of the chart are to be felt by the native concerned and in case the ascendant is weak or the longevity is less, the various effects of the chart would be of no use to the native. Next comes the strength of the Moon as only a sound mind can provide the native opportunities for rise in life. If the Moon is strong and has the help of a favorable Mercury and Jupiter, the native can make best use of opportunities available to him. The Moon is also the significator of mother and, if strong, it would bless the native with motherly comforts for proper development of life. Then comes the Sun and the ninth or fourth house, whichever contains first a mooltrikona sign, both factors related with father, who supports the native in the early years of life so to say till the child is competent to lead his/her own life. If the Sun, the ninth house and the fourth house are weak and afflicted, the father of the native has short life or lacks the power to support the native. In fact, if all these factors i.e. the ascendant, the Moon, the Sun, the ninth house and the fourth house are strong in a nativity, the native would get opportunities for advancement in life; so to say he/she has the capacity and chance to learn and to make use of it. Where there is no mooltrikona sign in the ninth and fourth houses, as happens with Libra ascendant, we examine about the father from the Sun and the influences on the ninth and fourth houses.

The planetary influences in the horoscope are studied through the natal conjunctions, aspects and placements. The conjunctions and aspects help us in identifying the auspicious and inauspicious planetary configurations. The placement of a planet in a particular house links the significations of its mooltrikona house with the significations of its house of placement. A planet placed in a malefic house indicates suffering for the significations ruled by the said planet in the nativity.

The integrated analytical technique will focus on a stepwise approach:

Step I

Double check the correctness of birth data. If any doubt persists, rectification should be done before anything else.

Step II

After the horoscope has been cast properly, identify the functional nature of the planets from the ascendant, the most effective point, the most malefic planet and the most benefic planet. Underline the functional malefic planets.

Step III

Find out the strength of planets, check to see if any planet is weak for several reasons, identify the natal auspicious and inauspicious close conjunctions/aspects and encircle planets/MEPs closely afflicted, identify the natal placements and have a comprehension of the weak and strong areas of the chart.

Step IV

Find out the current operating planetary periods (the main and sub-period) for the date in question. Identify the house where the mooltrikona sign of the sub-period lord is placed and the natal/transit houses occupied by the sub-period lord. In this approach we will primarily consider the sub-period lord.

Step V

For the triple transits on the date in question, find out the natal and transit strength of the sub-period lord and determine the triple transit triggering (TTT) influence i.e. from Transit to Natal, Transit to Transit, and Natal to Transit (not forgetting the special aspects of Mars, Jupiter, Saturn, Rahu and Ketu). Identify forthcoming TTT auspicious and inauspicious close influences also.

Step VI

Assess longevity: If a mooltrikona sign rises in the ascendant, pay special attention to the longevity by seeing the strength of planets and the functional nature of the operating planets i.e. the main and sub-period lords. Most of the planets being weak and afflictions to the ascendant or to the ascendant lord with operating period of functional malefic planets give short life. Similarly placed planets with operating period of functional benefic planets give middle span of life. Weak planets keep the significations to a lower level, if unafflicted. Severely afflicted planets cause tragedies or fatal diseases. The operating periods reduce/increase the impact. Pay special attention to the transit strength of operating planets.

For detailed study of the aspect of longevity, the readers may refer to Chapter 17 in our book, Systems' Approach For Interpreting Horoscopes.

Step VII

By using the sub periods and transits, combine these to see the current and future trends. Make your predictions for the different planetary periods.

Step VIII

Prescribe the astral remedies. The remedial measures are explained in Chapter 11.

Note: For various aspects of life, use the "Order of Seeing Significations" list in appendix. This list will assist you to identify the primary and secondary significators of various aspects of life.

The general assessment of the chart will indicate the significations of the houses/planets which will prominently surface in life depending upon the strength of planets. The specific trend results will be indicated at any particular time by the operating sub-period lord depending upon its functional nature and natal and transit strength. For analyzing any particular significations, strength of the house, the lord of the house and the significator of the house is considered. If the ascendant is having a mooltrikona sign and its lord is weak, the other weak planets show that the physical parts of the body ruled by such weak planets will suffer.

The house-wise analysis of horoscopes has been taken up by the authors in their book, "Systems' Approach for Interpreting Horoscopes". For the purpose of illustrations, we will take up some specific aspects of life in this book, which will give the readers a practical insight for analyzing a chart. The term, "the lord of the house" during the course of discussions on case studies refers always to the house where the mooltrikona sign of the said planet is placed i.e. its mooltrikona house.

Analysis of Mental Capabilities

Mental capabilities of a man like understanding, intelligence and analytic powers differentiate him from animals. The power of understanding helps in learning and power of analysis/ discrimination helps in developing innovative techniques and problem solving skills. The purpose of the human beings can only be achieved if they have mental capabilities. The brain is the part of the body which provides fruition of mental capabilities. Therefore the brain, which is ruled by the first house and the sign Aries, is the most important functional part of the human body. The power of understanding is governed by the strength of the third and fourth house and the Moon. The intelligence is governed by the fifth house and the Sun and the power of analysis/discrimination is governed by the strength of the planet Mercury.

The weakness of and affliction to the ascendant, the third, fourth and fifth houses, the Moon, the Sun and Mercury retard the growth of the mental capabilities and cause suffering to a native by denying the power of learning, acquiring intelligence and doing analytical work during the sub-period of weak and afflicted significators. The weakness of planets/houses only delays their results and makes them more vulnerable to natal and transit afflictions. Whereas affliction tries to destroy, deny and cause sufferings to their significations. On the functional and/or physical side, it causes diseases like epilepsy, brain hemorrhage, hydrocephalus, etc.

CHART 1

Male born 31st March, 1960, 0759 Hrs., Gurgaon, India.

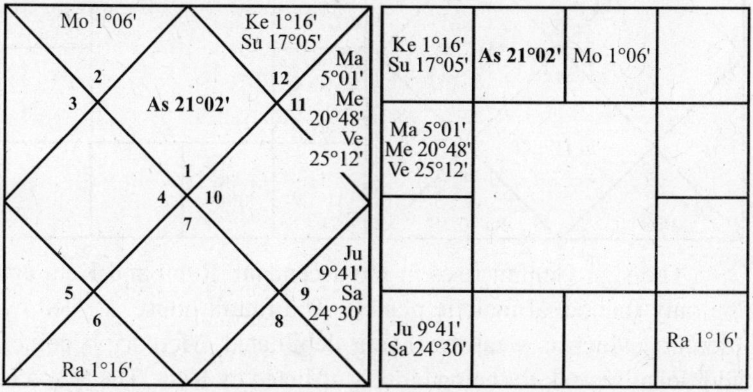

Mo 1°06'
2
3
As 21°02'
1
4
10
7
Ke 1°16'
Su 17°05'
12
11
Ma 5°01'
Me 20°48'
Ve 25°12'
5
6
Ra 1°16'
Ju 9°41'
9
Sa 24°30'
8

Ke 1°16' Su 17°05'	**As 21°02'**	Mo 1°06'	
Ma 5°01' Me 20°48' Ve 25°12'			
Ju 9°41' Sa 24°30'			Ra 1°16'

The sign Aries rises in the ascendant. Rahu, Ketu and Mercury become functional malefic planets. The lord of the ascendant turns weak due to the close affliction to the most effective point of the house of its placement. The lord of the fourth house, the Moon, is weak as it is in infancy and is exactly afflicted by Rahu from the sixth house. The lord of the fifth house, the Sun, is weak as it is badly placed. Mercury closely aspects and afflicts the most effective point of the fifth house. Saturn is weak as the most effective point of its mooltrikona house is closely afflicted by Mercury. Venus and Mercury are weak as their dispositor is weak and they are placed in an afflicted house. Jupiter is the only planet which is strong and placed in its own mooltrikona house. At birth the native was running the main period of the Sun, ruling the fifth house. The main period of the Sun was followed by the main period of the Moon, which is severely afflicted in the chart. The native could not study well and had to abandon his studies in school.

CHART 2

Male born 6th March, 1972, 1319 Hrs., New Delhi, India.

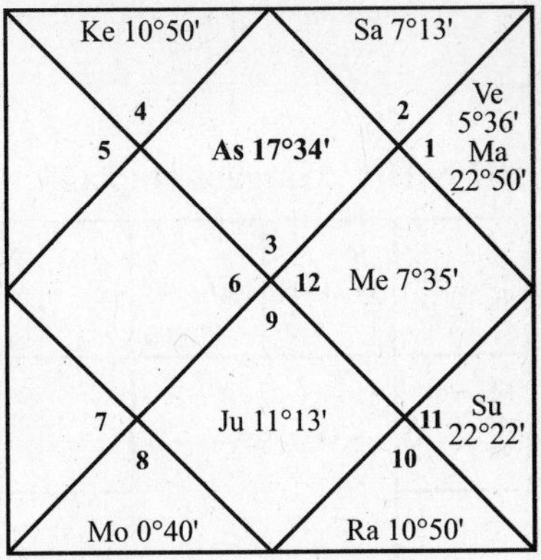

Ke 10°50' Sa 7°13'
4 2 Ve 5°36'
5 As 17°34' 1 Ma 22°50'
3
6 12 Me 7°35'
9
7 Ju 11°13' 11 Su 22°22'
8 10
Mo 0°40' Ra 10°50'

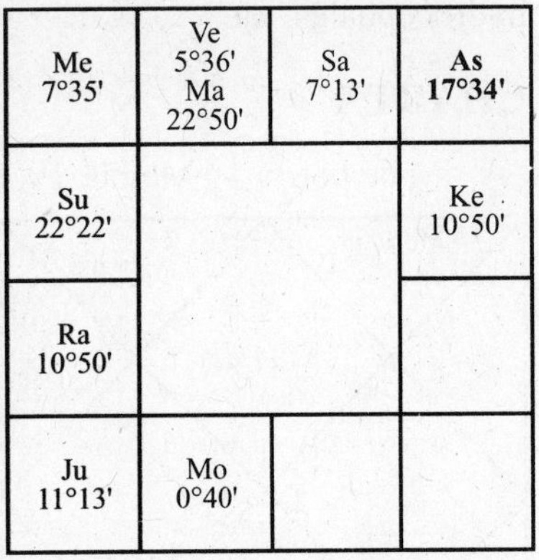

Me 7°35'	Ve 5°36' Ma 22°50'	Sa 7°13'	**As 17°34'**
Su 22°22'			Ke 10°50'
Ra 10°50'			
Ju 11°13'	Mo 0°40'		

The sign Gemini rises in the ascendant. Rahu and Ketu are the only functional malefic planets. The fourth house is ruled by Mercury which is weak for being debilitated. Mercury becomes additionally weak for being closely afflicted by Ketu. The Moon is absolutely weak as it is badly placed, debilitated and in extreme infancy. The Sun, representing understanding and intelligence, is weak as its dispositor is weak and afflicted. Saturn is weak as it is badly placed. It becomes additionally weak for being closely afflicted by Rahu from the eighth house. The Sun, the Moon and Mercury are all quite weak. When the native was of just ten months, the sub-period of Rahu in the main period of Jupiter started. Then the main period of weak and afflicted Saturn started. First of all, Saturn had its own sub-period in its own main period. The following sub-periods of weak and afflicted Mercury and of Ketu, which is afflicting Mercury, caused numerous health problems to the native and turned him mentally retarded. The parents, too, had fairly bad time as the fourth house, the ninth house, the Sun and the Moon representing parents, are all weak, and the lords of these houses are both afflicted.

CHART 3

Male born 5th December, 1976, 1005 Hrs., Bhiwani, India.

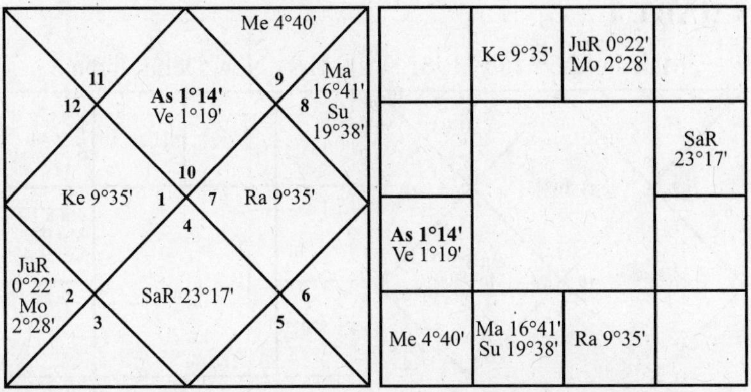

Me 4°40'
11
9
Ma 16°41'
12
As 1°14'
Ve 1°19'
8
Su 19°38'
10
Ke 9°35'
1
7
Ra 9°35'
4
JuR 0°22'
Mo 2°28'
2
SaR 23°17'
6
3
5

	Ke 9°35'	JuR 0°22' Mo 2°28'	
			SaR 23°17'
As 1°14' Ve 1°19'			
Me 4°40'	Ma 16°41' Su 19°38'	Ra 9°35'	

The sign Capricorn rises in the ascendant. Rahu, Ketu, the Sun and Jupiter become functional malefic planets. The Moon is weak as it is in infancy and the most effective point of its house of placement is exactly afflicted by Jupiter. It becomes additionally weak for being closely afflicted by Jupiter. Mercury is weak as it is badly placed, in infancy and occupies the mooltrikona sign of weak Jupiter. The mooltrikona sign of Mercury is also closely afflicted. Venus is weak as it is in infancy, it is exactly afflicted by Jupiter and its house of placement is also exactly afflicted. Saturn is weak as its dispositor is weak and afflicted. Jupiter is weak as it is in infancy, debilitated in navamsa and its house of placement is exactly afflicted by itself. Mars, being lord of the fourth house, is weak as it is combust and the most effective point of its house of placement is afflicted by Jupiter. Mars is additionally weak for being closely afflicted by the most malefic planet, the Sun. The Sun is weak as the most effective point of its house of placement is exactly afflicted by Jupiter. The most effective points of the ascendant and the fifth house are exactly afflicted by Jupiter. All factors, the ascendant, the Moon, Mercury, the Sun, the fourth house and the fifth house are weak. The native had the main period of the weak lord of the eighth house in operation at the time of birth followed by the main period of the weak and afflicted Moon and weak and afflicted Mars. The native had retarded physical and mental growth.

CHART 4

Male born 3rd July, 1981, 1500 Hrs., New Delhi, India.

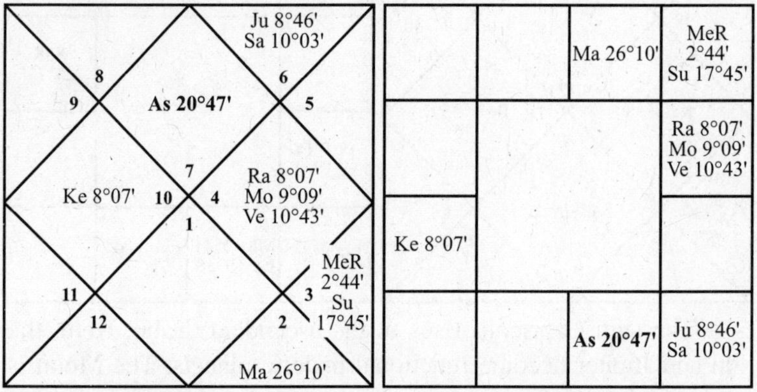

Ju 8°46'
Sa 10°03'
8
6
9
As 20°47'
5
7
Ra 8°07'
Mo 9°09'
Ve 10°43'
Ke 8°07'
10
4
1
MeR
2°44'
Su
17°45'
11
3
12
2
Ma 26°10'

		Ma 26°10'	MeR 2°44' Su 17°45'
			Ra 8°07' Mo 9°09' Ve 10°43'
Ke 8°07'			
		As 20°47'	Ju 8°46' Sa 10°03'

The sign Libra rises in the ascendant. Rahu, Ketu and Mercury become functional malefic planets. The Moon is weak as it is closely afflicted by Rahu and Ketu. Venus, the lord of the ascendant, is weak as its dispositor is weak and afflicted. Venus becomes additionally weak for being closely afflicted by the Rahu-Ketu axis. Jupiter, ruling growth, is weak as it is badly placed, occupies the mooltrikona sign of weak Mercury and is exactly afflicted by Ketu. Saturn, ruling intelligence, is weak as it is badly placed, debilitated in navamsa and its dispositor is weak. Saturn becomes additionally weak for being closely afflicted by Ketu. Mercury is weak as it is in infancy. Mars is weak as it is badly placed and in old age. The Sun is the only strong planet in this nativity. The sub-periods of Venus, the Moon, Mars and Rahu in the main period of badly placed and afflicted Saturn were detrimental to the physical and mental health of the child. The next main period of the functional malefic planet, Mercury did not indicate any improvement. The child was mentally retarded and had been a hydrocephalic and underwent many surgical operations. The native saw the end of life in the sub-period of Mercury in its own main period after experiencing all types of physical sufferings.

CHART 5

Male born 10th January, 1983, 1252 Hrs., New Delhi, India.

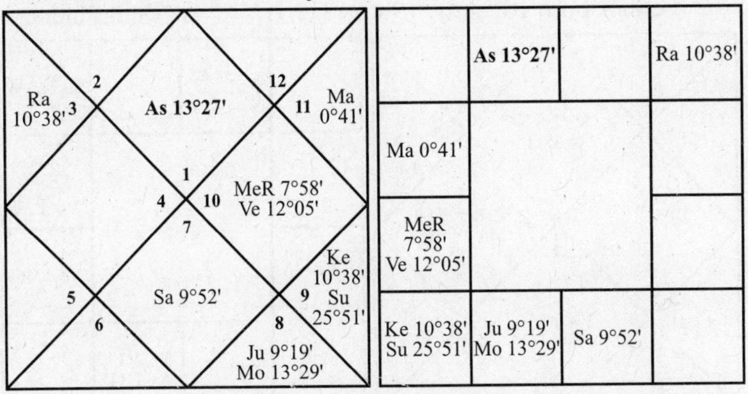

2
Ra 10°38' 3
As 13°27'
12
11 Ma 0°41'
1
4
10 MeR 7°58' Ve 12°05'
7
Ke 10°38'
5
Sa 9°52'
9 Su 25°51'
6
8
Ju 9°19' Mo 13°29'

	As 13°27'		Ra 10°38'
Ma 0°41'			
MeR 7°58' Ve 12°05'			
Ke 10°38' Su 25°51'	Ju 9°19' Mo 13°29'	Sa 9°52'	

The sign Aries rises in the ascendant. Rahu, Ketu and Mercury become functional malefic planets. The lord of the ascendant, Mars, is weak as it is in infancy and its dispositor is weak due to exact affliction. Saturn is weak as it is exactly afflicted by Rahu. Rahu and Ketu are close to the most effective point of the houses of their location and afflict all the houses occupied and aspected, except the seventh house as Venus is strong. Mercury, ruling analytical power, is weak as it is debilitated in navamsa. The Moon, ruling the fourth house, is weak as it is badly placed, debilitated in birth chart and debilitated in navamsa. Jupiter is weak as it is badly placed. The Sun, ruling the fifth house and intelligence, is weak as it is placed in an afflicted house and its dispositor is weak. At birth the native was in the sub-period of Rahu in the main period of weak and afflicted, Saturn. This was followed by the sub-period of weak Jupiter. These sub-periods posed many health problems to the native. During the sub-period of Mercury in its own main period the child started suffering from epileptic fits, which were aggravated in the following sub-period of Ketu. The propitiatory and strengthening remedial measures were suggested for the afflicting and weak planets, respectively, to prevent recurrence of fits. The performance of astral remedies did show improvement but the mental growth of the child remained semi-retarded.

CHART 6

Female born 10th July, 1986, 1312 Hrs., New Delhi, India.

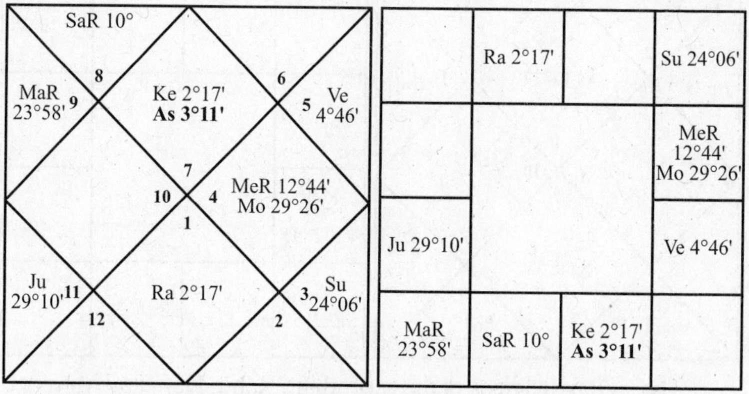

SaR 10°
8
MaR 23°58' 9
Ke 2°17' **As 3°11'**
6
5 Ve 4°46'
7
10
4
MeR 12°44' Mo 29°26'
1
Ju 29°10' 11
Ra 2°17'
3 Su 24°06'
12
2

	Ra 2°17'		Su 24°06'
			MeR 12°44' Mo 29°26'
Ju 29°10'			Ve 4°46'
MaR 23°58'	SaR 10°	Ke 2°17' **As 3°11'**	

The sign Libra rises in the ascendant. Rahu, Ketu and Mercury become functional malefic planets. Venus, the lord of the ascendant, is weak as it is placed in an afflicted house and the ascendant is afflicted by the Rahu-Ketu axis within an orb of one degree. Rahu and Ketu are close to the most effective point of the houses of their location and afflict all the houses occupied and aspected including the ascendant. The Moon is weak as it is in old-age, and becomes additionally weak for being closely afflicted by Rahu. Saturn, ruling intellect, is weak as the most effective point of its mooltrikona house is exactly afflicted by Ketu. Mercury, ruling analytical power, is weak as its dispositor is weak. Jupiter ruling growth is weak as it is in old-age and its dispositor is weak. The child was born in the main period of functional malefic planet, Mercury. During early childhood, she remained mentally retarded and was suffering from epileptic fits. The propitiatory and strengthening remedial measures were suggested for the afflicting and weak planets, respectively. The performance of the astral remedies did show improvement.

CHART 7

Male born 3rd October, 1988, 0130 Hrs., New Delhi, India.

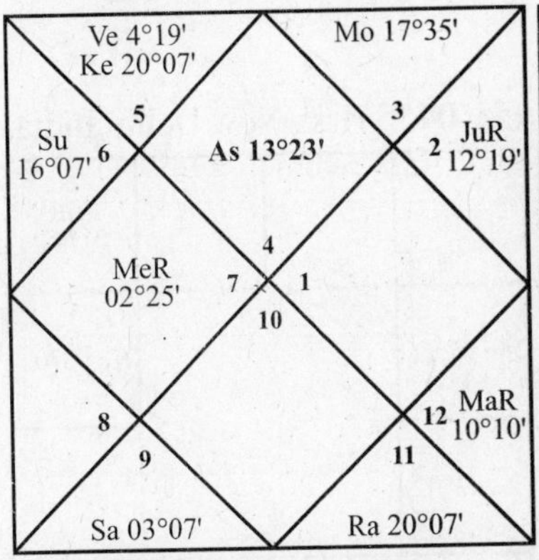

Ve 4°19'
Ke 20°07'
Mo 17°35'
5
3
Su
16°07' 6
As 13°23'
2 JuR
12°19'
4
MeR
02°25' 7
1
10
8
12 MaR
10°10'
9
11
Sa 03°07'
Ra 20°07'

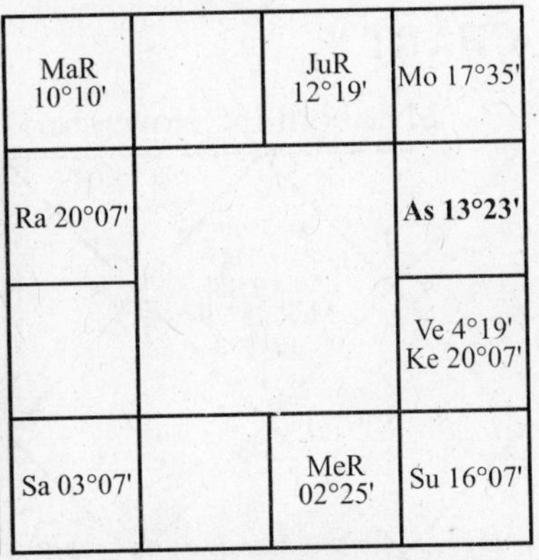

MaR 10°10'		JuR 12°19'	Mo 17°35'
Ra 20°07'			As 13°23'
			Ve 4°19' Ke 20°07'
Sa 03°07'		MeR 02°25'	Su 16°07'

The sign Cancer rises in the ascendant. Rahu, Ketu, Jupiter and Saturn become functional malefic planets. The Moon, being lord of the ascendant, is weak as it is badly placed. It becomes additionally weak as it is closely afflicted by Rahu from the eighth house. The lord of the third house, Mercury, ruling growth is weak as it is in infancy, its dispositor is weak and the most effective point of its mooltrikona house is afflicted by Jupiter. The Sun is weak as its dispositor is weak and the most effective point of its house of placement is exactly afflicted by Jupiter. The Sun becomes additionally weak as it is closely afflicted by Jupiter. Venus, the lord of the fourth house, too, is weak as its dispositor is weak. The most effective points of the eleventh, third, fifth and seventh houses are exactly afflicted by Jupiter. The third and eleventh houses rule ears. The exact affliction to the most effective points of these houses with weakness of the third lord turned the child deaf and dumb which resulted in mental retardation. The child was born in the sub-period of the weak and afflicted Sun in the main period of Rahu. The child started suffering from epileptic fits. The propitiatory and strengthening remedial measures were suggested for the afflicting and weak planets, respectively. The performance of the astrological remedial measures did show some improvement in the case of epileptic fits. The child also started responding to the treatment for his dumbness.

CHART 8

Male born 15th November, 1953, 0455 Hrs., New Delhi, India.

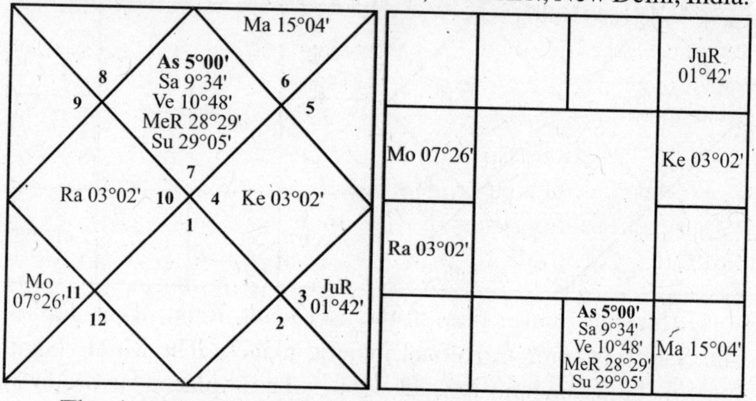

Ma 15°04'
8 As 5°00' Sa 9°34' Ve 10°48' MeR 28°29' Su 29°05' 6
9 5
7
Ra 03°02' 10 4 Ke 03°02'
1
Mo 07°26' 11 3 JuR 01°42'
12 2

			JuR 01°42'
Mo 07°26'			Ke 03°02'
Ra 03°02'			
		As 5°00' Sa 9°34' Ve 10°48' MeR 28°29' Su 29°05'	Ma 15°04'

The sign Libra rises in the ascendant. Rahu, Ketu and Mercury become functional malefic planets. Rahu and Ketu are close to the most effective point of the houses of their location and afflict all the houses occupied and aspected including the fourth and sixth houses. Mercury, ruling analytical faculties, is weak as it is combust and in old-age. The debilitated and old-aged Sun is exactly afflicted by Mercury. The Moon is weak as the most effective point of its mooltrikona house is under the multiple affliction of Rahu-Ketu axis within an orb of two degrees. Jupiter, ruling the house of growth, is weak as it is in infancy. The lords of the first and the fifth houses are strong in this chart. The native first experienced mental ill health during the sub-period of Mercury in the main period of Rahu as Mercury is closely afflicting the weak Sun. Slowly the native started suffering from epileptic fits. The strength of Venus and Saturn helped the native through medication and the performance of astrological remedial measures.

Analysis of a Chart for Heart Disease

The medical astrology, which is a branch of astrology, is one of the various facets of the divine science of astrology for the benefit of the mankind and it is fully competent to answer our questions regarding health that is (1) to what type of diseases a native may be vulnerable to; (2) when; (3) whether it will respond to medical treatment; and (4) preventive measures. The analysis based on Systems' Approach clearly indicates the status of health. The health is one of the various aspects of life and heart disease is a part thereof. The natal chart of a person can indicate whether a person is likely to have a heart disease and if so, at what age. For detailed study of the status of health, the readers may refer to our book, "A Complete Book on Medical Astrology".

First of all we identify the planets. The lord of the ascendant and/or the lord of the sixth house containing a mooltrikona sign is/are the prime indicators of health. The lord of the fourth house is the secondary indicator so far as the heart disease is concerned. The planets, the Sun and the Moon are the primary and secondary significators for a heart disease, respectively. The Moon governs the blood and represents all functions in human body. Other contributory planets are Mars, ruling the muscular parts, and Jupiter, governing the arteries.

If the prime indicators and/or the fourth house containing a mooltrikona sign are weak and the most effective points of the first, sixth and/or fourth houses are afflicted, the person would be vulnerable to a heart disease.

Since the Moon and Mercury are weak quite often and, in case of Aries rising, the Moon becomes secondary indicator/ significator for heart condition and Mercury becomes prime indicator of health, it makes Arians vulnerable to heart problems if Mars too is weak. Such natives would better use preventive astral remedies to take care.

Examining the Operational Planets

The close conjunction/aspect of the functional malefic planets with the weak prime indicator(s) of health and/or the primary or secondary significators for a heart disease will indicate the heart disease in the operational sub-periods of the functional malefic planets in the periods of weak prime indicator(s) and/or weak significators at an early stage of life. The indications of the timing are given also by the operating sub-periods of weak and afflicted prime indicators of health and/or weak and afflicted primary or secondary significators.

The involvement of Mars as functional malefic planet, the lord of the sixth house ruling injuries and Ketu create the eventualities for operations and the absence of their involvement enables the native to respond to symptomatic treatment.

The effect of the triple transit triggering influence of functional malefic planets is seen over the natal/transit weak indicators meticulously to forewarn the person.

Let us study the matter further through some case studies:

CHART 9

Male born 24th December, 1968, 0634 Hrs. at Gurgaon, India.

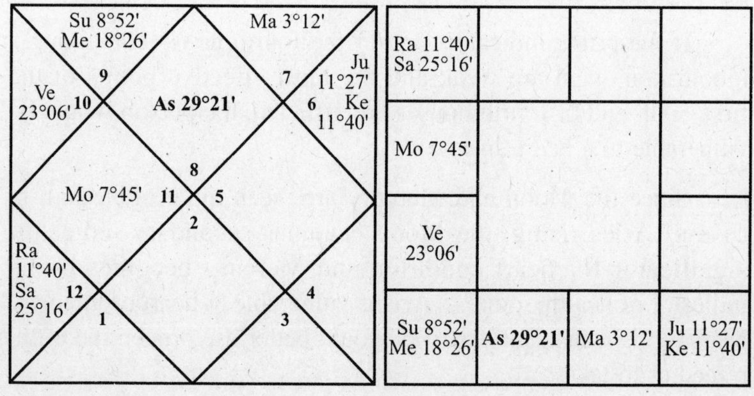

The sign Scorpio rises in the ascendant. Rahu, Ketu, Mars and Venus become functional malefic planets. Jupiter significator for arteries is under exact affliction of Rahu and Ketu. The Sun is also subjected to the same affliction as the Sun is placed in the mooltrikona sign of Jupiter. Mars as prime determinant of health is also weak due to bad placement. The lord of fourth house is weak as it is placed in an afflicted house. During the sub period of the Sun in April, 2012, when the prolonged stationary influence of Rahu and Ketu afflicted the natal Jupiter, Rahu and Ketu the native suffered from a heart attack and had to undergo an open heart surgery. The native was suggested continuous performance of propitiatory remedial measures for the afflicting planets and strengthening measures for the weak planets. The weakness of Jupiter does not allow the person to follow astral remedies advice, as prescribed.

CHART 10

Male born 29th August, 1948, 2330 Hrs. at New Delhi, India.

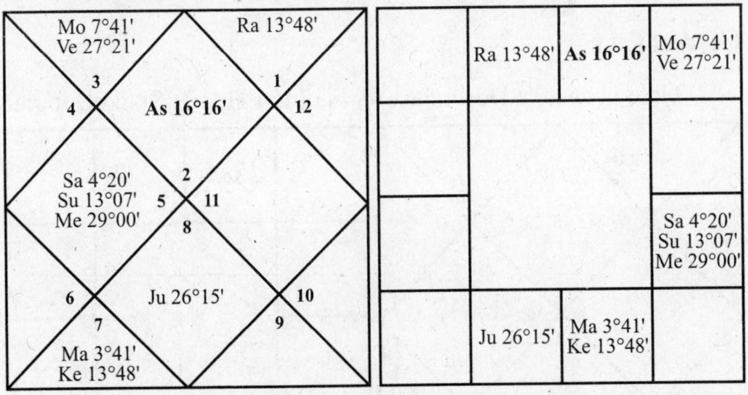

Mo 7°41' Ve 27°21' (3)
Ra 13°48' (1)
4 **As 16°16'** 12
2
Sa 4°20' Su 13°07' Me 29°00' (5)
11
8
6 Ju 26°15' 10
7 9
Ma 3°41' Ke 13°48'

	Ra 13°48'	**As 16°16'**	Mo 7°41' Ve 27°21'
			Sa 4°20' Su 13°07' Me 29°00'
	Ju 26°15'	Ma 3°41' Ke 13°48'	

The sign Taurus rises in the ascendant. Rahu, Ketu, Venus, Jupiter and Mars become functional malefic planets. Mars is weak as it is badly placed, is in infancy and its dispositor is weak. Mars is additionally weak as its mooltrikona house and house of placement are both closely afflicted by the Rahu-Ketu axis. Rahu and Ketu are close to the most effective point of the houses of their location and afflict all the houses occupied and aspected, including the most effective points of the fourth and sixth houses. The primary significator and secondary indicator, the Sun, is exactly afflicted by Rahu from the twelfth house. The Moon is weak as the most effective point of its house of placement is closely afflicted by Ketu from the sixth house. Venus, ruling the sixth house and becoming the prime indicator of health, is weak as it is in old-age and its mooltrikona house is closely afflicted by the Rahu-Ketu axis. Saturn, placed in the fourth house, is weak as it is combust, in infancy and its dispositor is weak and afflicted. Saturn becomes additionally weak as the most effective points of its mooltrikona house and house of placement are closely afflicted by Ketu and Rahu, respectively, and both from malefic houses. Whenever a functional malefic planet afflicts another planet/house from a malefic house its impact is further aggravated. During the sub-period of Venus, ruling the afflicted sixth house, and in the main period of Saturn, the native suffered a massive heart attack and died within a few minutes.

CHART 11

Male born 13th December, 1944, 1454 Hrs. at Sialkot, India.

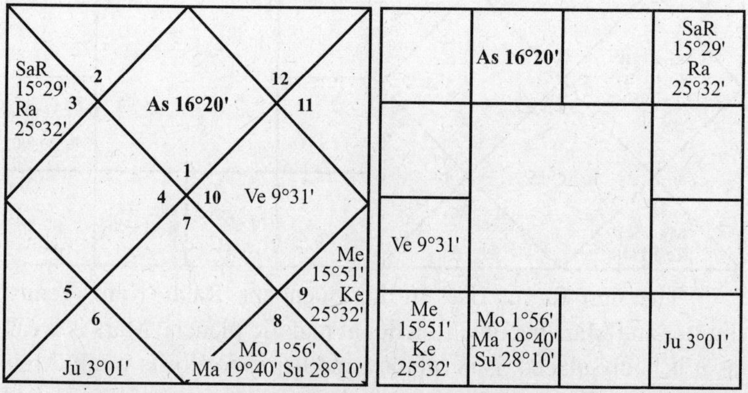

SaR 15°29' Ra 25°32'
2
3
12
As 16°20'
11
1
4
10
Ve 9°31'
7
Me 15°51' Ke 25°32'
5
9
6
8
Mo 1°56'
Ju 3°01'
Ma 19°40' Su 28°10'

	As 16°20'		SaR 15°29' Ra 25°32'
Ve 9°31'			
Me 15°51' Ke 25°32'	Mo 1°56' Ma 19°40' Su 28°10'		Ju 3°01'

The sign Aries rises in the ascendant. Rahu, Ketu and Mercury become functional malefic planets. Mars is weak as it is combust and badly placed. Mercury is weak as its dispositor is weak. Jupiter is weak as it is badly placed, its mooltrikona sign is afflicted, it is in infancy and debilitated in navamsa. The Moon is weak as it is badly placed, debilitated, in infancy and lacks full luster. The Sun is weak as it is badly placed and in old-age. The prime indicators of health, Mars and Mercury; the secondary indicator, the Moon, and the significators, the Sun and the Moon are all weak. During the main period of the functional malefic planet, Ketu, and the sub-period of the functional malefic planet, Mercury, the native suffered from heart problem and underwent open heart surgery in the beginning of the main period of Venus. Venus is strong in the birth chart which helped the native.

CHART 12

Male born 10th August, 1947, 2256 Hrs. at Kolkata, India.

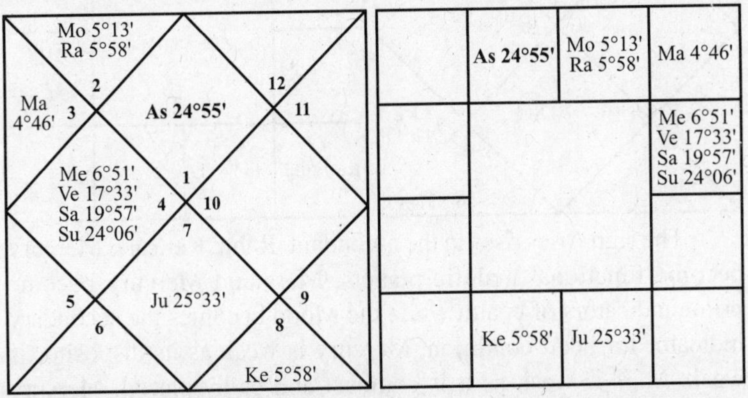

Mo 5°13'
Ra 5°58'
2
12
Ma
4°46' 3
As 24°55'
11
Me 6°51'
Ve 17°33'
Sa 19°57'
Su 24°06'
1
4
10
7
5
Ju 25°33'
9
6
8
Ke 5°58'

	As 24°55'	Mo 5°13' Ra 5°58'	Ma 4°46'
			Me 6°51' Ve 17°33' Sa 19°57' Su 24°06'
	Ke 5°58'	Ju 25°33'	

The sign Aries rises in the ascendant . Rahu, Ketu and Mercury become functional malefic planets. Mars and Mercury become prime indicators of health while the Moon becomes the secondary indicator for heart condition. Mars is fairly strong. The Moon is weak as it is exactly afflicted by functional malefic planets, Rahu and Ketu. Mercury is weak as its dispositor is weak and it is afflicted by the exact aspect of Ketu from the eighth house. The Sun is weak as its dispositor is weak and afflicted. Jupiter is weak as its dispositor is weak. The close affliction to the lord of the fourth house and the lord of the sixth house in the fourth house resulted in a heart attack in the sub-period of Ketu in the main period of Jupiter. At the time of the heart problem, the natal Mars was under the close transit affliction of stationary Ketu and Rahu, but as the lord of the ascendant is not under severe affliction in the birth chart, the native responded to the symptomatic treatment.

CHART 13

Male born 3rd April, 1964, 0750 Hrs. at Ferozepur, India.

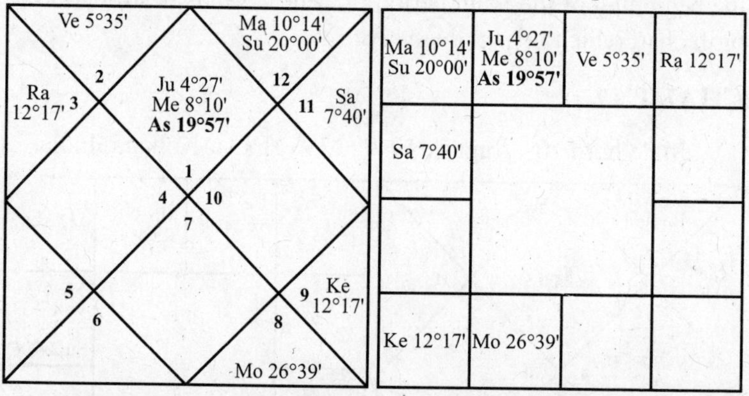

Ve 5°35'
Ma 10°14'
Su 20°00'
2
12
Ra 12°17' 3
Ju 4°27'
Me 8°10'
As 19°57'
11 Sa 7°40'
1
4 10
7
5
9 Ke 12°17'
6
8
Mo 26°39'

Ma 10°14' Su 20°00'	Ju 4°27' Me 8°10' **As 19°57'**	Ve 5°35'	Ra 12°17'
Sa 7°40'			
Ke 12°17'	Mo 26°39'		

The sign Aries rises in the ascendant .Rahu, Ketu and Mercury become functional malefic planets. Mars and Mercury become prime indicators of health while the Moon becomes the secondary indicator for heart condition. Mercury is weak as its dispositor is weak. Mars is weak as it is combust and badly placed. Mercury becomes additionally weak by being closely afflicted by Ketu. The Sun, being primary significator of the heart, is weak as it is badly placed. The Moon, being prime indicator of heart condition, is very weak as it is badly placed, debilitated and in old-age. The several weaknesses and afflictions make the native vulnerable to heart problems during transit afflictions in the sub-periods of indicator and significator planets. The native suffered from heart disease and had to undergo an open heart surgery at the young age of 27 years, in the sub-period of Mercury in the main period of Venus.

Analysis of Pre-Marital Pleasures

Inclinations for sensual or lascivious pleasures stem from strong emotional nature and courage. The fifth house, its lord and the Moon govern the emotions and make a person highly emotional by their influence on the ascendant, the fifth or the seventh houses. The third lord, Mars and Rahu govern the courage. Rahu and the lords of the twelfth and eighth houses signify cravings for pleasures and for sensual pleasures when closely connected with Venus, the Moon, the eighth house, the ascendant or the seventh house. Rahu, Venus and the lord of the eighth house when connected with the factors of emotions and courage give passions for love during their operating sub-periods and the natives strive for the fulfillment of desires of sensual pleasures leaving all social norms, disregarding the age of the person, whether an unmarried youth or a young person or one in advanced age and disregarding the sex of the person whether a male or a female. The weakness of Jupiter and ninth house are additional contributing factors. The close influence of Rahu on factors governing sexual matters usually gives lust and seldom results in marriage with the partner involved in such affairs. The placement of the fifth lord in the seventh or eighth house or vice-versa gives primarily deep inclinations for sensual pleasures. Delay in marriage due to weakness of the prime indicators of marriage and afflictions, give rise to pre-marital affairs. Under the Systems' Approach, the lordship attributed to each planet always refers to the mooltrikona house of that planet only and influence means a close conjunction or a close aspect. The analysis is made only with reference to ascendant.

Let us discuss the matter further with the help of some case studies:

CHART 14

Female born 28th October, 1971, 0805 Hrs. at New Delhi, India.

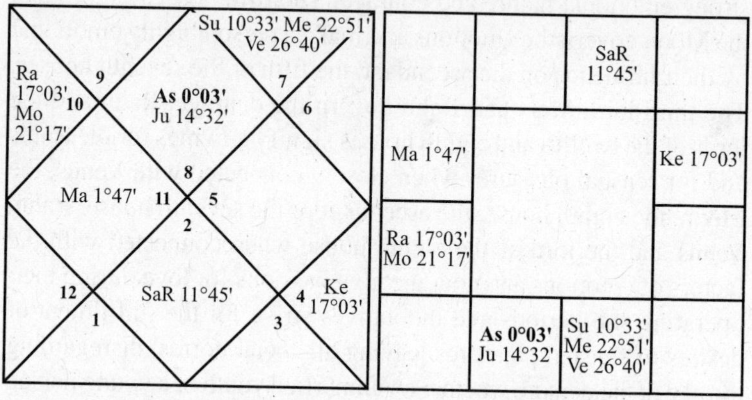

Su 10°33' Me 22°51' Ve 26°40'
7
6
Ra 17°03'
Mo 21°17'
9
10
As 0°03'
Ju 14°32'
8
Ma 1°47'
11
5
2
12
SaR 11°45'
4
Ke 17°03'
1
3

		SaR 11°45'	
Ma 1°47'			Ke 17°03'
Ra 17°03' Mo 21°17'			
	As 0°03' Ju 14°32'	Su 10°33' Me 22°51' Ve 26°40'	

The sign Scorpio rises in the ascendant. Rahu, Ketu, Mars and Venus become functional malefic planets. The Moon, governing the emotions, is under the close influence of Rahu, in the third house ruling initiatives. Mars closely exerts its influence on the fourth, seventh, tenth and eleventh houses. The Sun is weak as it is badly placed and debilitated. Mercury is weak as it is combust, badly placed and afflicted. Venus is fairly strong. The lord of the fourth house, ruling the chastity, is weak as it is debilitated in navamsa. The Sun, Mercury and Saturn are additionally weak as the most effective points of their mooltrikona houses are closely afflicted by Mars. Saturn is additionally weak as the most effective point of its house of placement is also closely afflicted by Mars. The Sun, ruling the will power, is very weak in the nativity. During the sub-period of Mercury in the main period of Rahu, the girl eloped with a boy even before attaining the age of 18 years.

CHART 15

Female born 16th June, 1964, 1630 Hrs. at New Delhi, India.

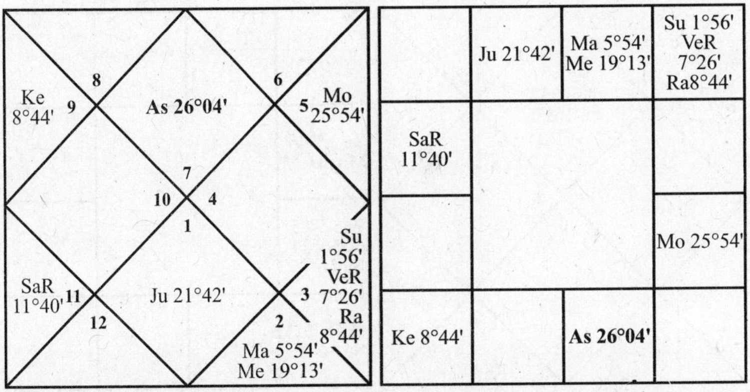

8
Ke 8°44' 9
As 26°04'
6
5 Mo 25°54'
7
10 4
1
SaR 11°40' 11
Ju 21°42'
12
3 Su 1°56' VeR 7°26' Ra 8°44'
2
Ma 5°54' Me 19°13'

	Ju 21°42'	Ma 5°54' Me 19°13'	Su 1°56' VeR 7°26' Ra8°44'
SaR 11°40'			
			Mo 25°54'
Ke 8°44'		**As 26°04'**	

The sign Libra rises in the ascendant . Rahu, Ketu and Mercury become functional malefic planets. The lord of the third house, Jupiter, closely influences the most effective points of the seventh, eleventh, first and third houses. The planet of emotions, the Moon, exactly aspects and influences the most effective point of the fifth house. The lords of the twelfth and seventh houses are placed in the eighth house. Rahu closely influences the lord of the ascendant and the lord of the fifth house. All these influences on emotional aspects and on the eighth house created deep interests in intimate relationships with the opposite sex. During the sub-period of Venus in the main period of Mars, the native had fallen in love, which was, in fact a short lived involvement. Rahu's influence on Venus only resulted in cravings for physical pleasures.

CHART 16

Female born 1st January, 1963, 0646 Hrs. at New Delhi, India.

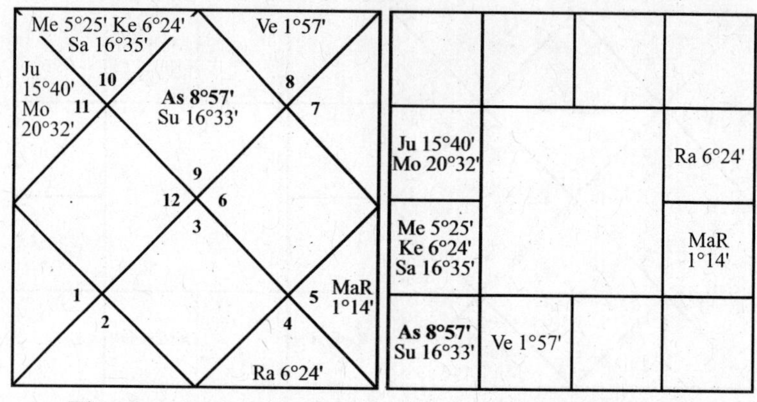

The sign Sagittarius rises in the ascendant. Rahu, Ketu and the Moon become functional malefic planets. The most effective points of the eighth, twelfth, second and fourth houses and the planets Venus and Mercury are under the close influence of Rahu. The lord of the eighth house and the significator for emotions, the Moon, exerts influence on the lord of the ascendant in the third house. During the sub-period of Venus in the main period of Saturn, the lord of the third house, the native was involved in a love affair with a boy of another caste. The affair was short lived as the weak Venus is influenced by Rahu.

CHART 17

Female born 25th March, 1958, 1207 Hrs. at New Delhi, India.

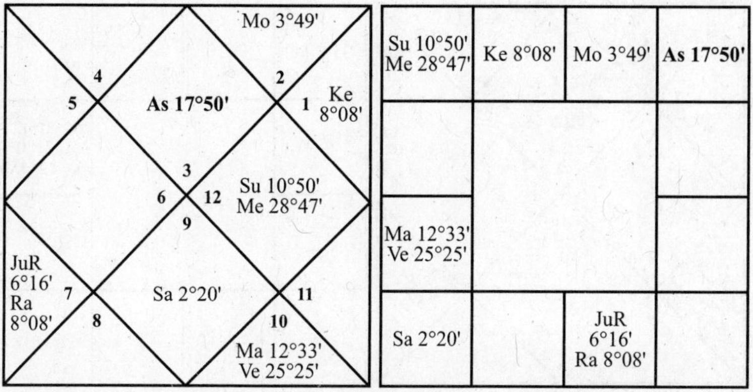

Mo 3°49'
4
2
5
As 17°50'
1
Ke 8°08'
3
6
12
Su 10°50'
Me 28°47'
9
JuR 6°16'
Ra 8°08'
7
Sa 2°20'
11
8
10
Ma 12°33'
Ve 25°25'

Su 10°50' Me 28°47'	Ke 8°08'	Mo 3°49'	**As 17°50'**
Ma 12°33' Ve 25°25'			
Sa 2°20'		JuR 6°16' Ra 8°08'	

The sign Gemini rises in the ascendant. Rahu and Ketu are the functional malefic planets. The lord of the seventh house is in the fifth house and is under the close influence of Rahu. Mercury, ruling the fourth house, is weak as it is in old-age and is debilitated. The lord of the fifth house, Venus, is placed in the eighth house. The lord of the eleventh house, ruling friends, is also in the eighth house. The prime significators for marriage in this case being Jupiter, the Moon and Mercury are all weak which caused delay in marriage. The delay in marriage and the involvement of the lord of the seventh house with Rahu gives uncontrolled passions and intense inclinations for sensual pleasures. The delay in marriage resulted in a very long spell of a pre-marital affair with a boy of another faith. The affair started in the sub-period of Jupiter in the main period of Rahu.

CHART 18

Female born 22nd June, 1966, 0900 Hrs. at New Delhi, India.

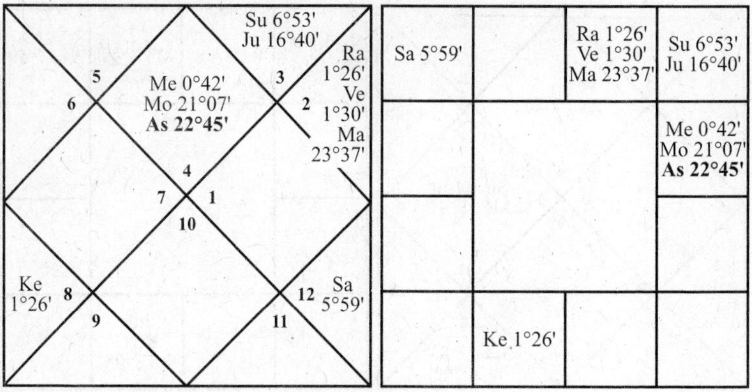

Su 6°53' Ju 16°40'
5 6 Me 0°42' Mo 21°07' **As 22°45'** 3 2 Ra 1°26' Ve 1°30' Ma 23°37'
4 7 1 10
Ke 1°26' 8 9 12 Sa 5°59' 11

Sa 5°59'		Ra 1°26' Ve 1°30' Ma 23°37'	Su 6°53' Ju 16°40'
			Me 0°42' Mo 21°07' **As 22°45'**
	Ke 1°26'		

The sign Cancer rises in the ascendant. Rahu, Ketu, Jupiter and Saturn become functional malefic planets. The significator of the emotions, ruling the ascendant, closely influences the most effective point of the ascendant and the seventh house. The lord of the third house is under the close influence of Ketu from the fifth house. The lord of the second house is badly placed in the twelfth house along with Jupiter. Venus, the lord of the fourth house, is exactly conjunct with Rahu. The affliction of the lord of the fourth house and the bad placement of the lord of the second house could not give an early marriage but the influence of Rahu to Venus gave intense desires for gratification of sensual pleasures. The girl had an affair in the sub-period of Rahu in the main period of the Ketu at the age of 15 years and in the 16th year she eloped with her paramour.

CHART 19

Male born 6th August, 1959, 0235 Hrs. at Gurgaon, India.

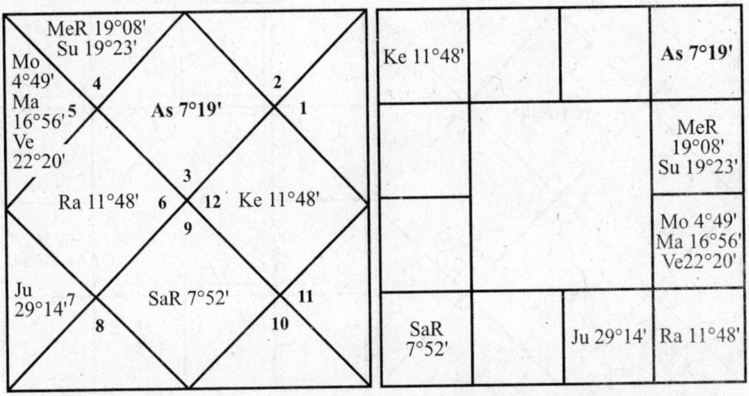

MeR 19°08'
Su 19°23'
Mo 4°49'
Ma 16°56'
Ve 22°20'
4
5
As 7°19'
2
1
3
Ra 11°48' 6
12 Ke 11°48'
9
Ju 29°14' 7
8
SaR 7°52'
11
10

Ke 11°48'			As 7°19'
			MeR 19°08' Su 19°23'
			Mo 4°49' Ma 16°56' Ve22°20'
SaR 7°52'		Ju 29°14'	Ra 11°48'

The sign Gemini rises in the ascendant. Rahu, Ketu are the functional malefic planets. The lord of the fourth house is closely conjunct with the lord of the third house in the second house. The lord of the seventh house is placed in the house of emotions. Jupiter is weak as it is in old-age. There are three planets in the third house including Mars. The Moon ruling emotions closely influences the most effective point of the third house. This indicates the native has intense emotions and takes initiative in this regard. The weakness of the lord of the seventh, second and fourth houses delayed the marriage and the native could not resist the emotional initiatives. The native had many emotional involvements during the sub-periods of the Moon, Mars and Rahu in the main period of the Sun and was finally married in the sub-period of the Jupiter with a girl of his choice after a pre-marital love affair.

CHART 20

Male born 15th June, 1961, 1049 Hrs. at New Delhi, India.

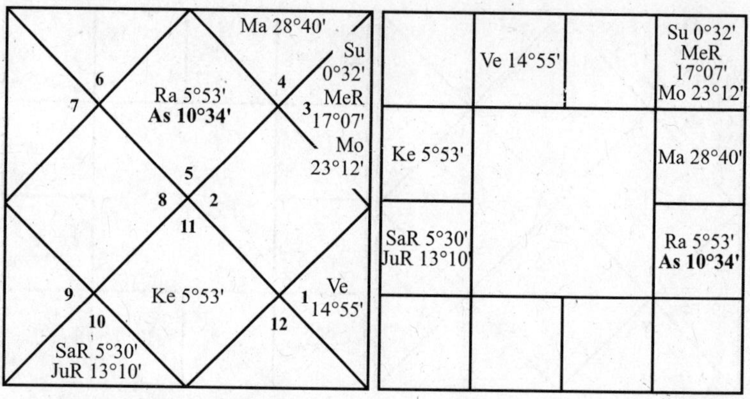

Ma 28°40'
Su 0°32' MeR 17°07' Mo 23°12'
6 7 4 3
Ra 5°53' **As 10°34'**
5 8 2 11
9 Ke 5°53' 1 Ve 14°55'
10 12
SaR 5°30' JuR 13°10'

	Ve 14°55'		Su 0°32' MeR 17°07' Mo 23°12'
Ke 5°53'			Ma 28°40'
SaR 5°30' JuR 13°10'			Ra 5°53' **As 10°34'**

The sign Leo rises in the ascendant. Rahu, Ketu and the Moon become functional malefic planets. The lord of the third house, Venus, closely influences the most effective point of the third house. The lord of the fifth house is weak as it is debilitated and badly placed. The lord of the seventh house is weak as it is badly placed in the sixth house ruling conflicts. The Sun, ruling the ascendant, is weak as it is in the state of infancy in the chart and debilitated in navamsa. When Rahu occupies the ascendant and its lord is weak, Rahu influences the personality of the native to be a pleasure seeker. During the sub-period of the Moon, ruling the emotions, in the main period of the lord of the seventh house, the native was emotionally involved. The marriage of the native was finalized with his beloved after lot of problems. The marital relationship continued with persistent conflicts as both the lords of the fifth and seventh houses are placed in the house of conflicts.

CHART 21

Female born 30th August, 1968, 1609 Hrs. at New Delhi, India.

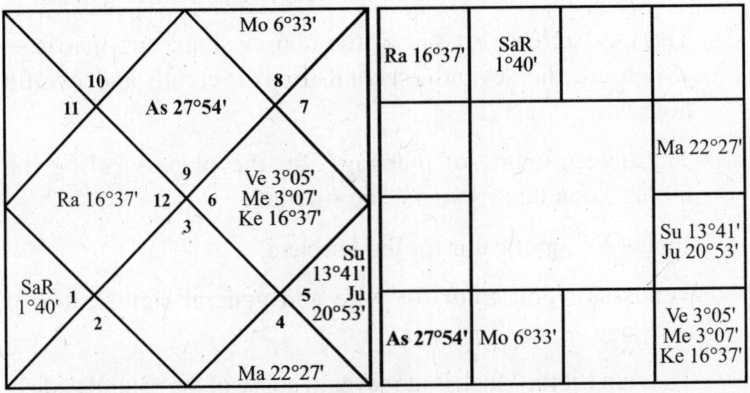

Mo 6°33'
10
8
11
As 27°54'
7
9
Ve 3°05'
Ra 16°37' 12
6 Me 3°07'
3
Ke 16°37'
Su
13°41'
SaR 1
5 Ju
1°40'
20°53'
2
4
Ma 22°27'

Ra 16°37'	SaR 1°40'		
			Ma 22°27'
			Su 13°41' Ju 20°53'
As 27°54'	Mo 6°33'		Ve 3°05' Me 3°07' Ke 16°37'

The sign Sagittarius rises in the ascendant. Rahu, Ketu and the Moon become functional malefic planets. The lord of the fifth house is debilitated and is placed in the eighth house. The planets placed in the eighth house give inclinations for indulgence in sex. The lord of the third house is placed in the fifth house. The lord of the eighth house is debilitated and badly placed in the twelfth house, indicating deep interests in carnal pleasures. Venus is weak as it is debilitated and is in infancy. As the Moon is the prime determinant for marriage for Sagittarians, its weakness delayed the marriage and the native was involved in so called love affairs to satisfy her urges for carnal pleasures.

Analysing Marital Discord

Marital discord is a universal problem all over the world. The reasons can be many including the economical, lack of physical and psychological compatibility, extra-marital relations, aggressive attitude of husband/wife, selfish nature of the husband/wife, etc. There are marriages which survive in spite of all the problems mentioned above with some amount of inharmonious relationship and yet there are others which cannot bear the strains and end in divorce. The reasons can be traced to the operating sub-period of the planet indicating marital discord. The problems in marriage are shown by the affliction(s) caused by the functional malefic planet(s) to one or more of the following weak planets/houses:

- The most effective point of the houses signifying marriage, which are the seventh, second, fourth, eighth and twelfth houses.
- The determinants of marriage i.e. the planets ruling the mooltrikona houses signifying marriage.
- Jupiter as significator for the husband.
- Venus as significator for wife and general significator of marriage.
- The sign Libra, which is the seventh house of the natural zodiac.

The weak planets delay the marriage while the close or exact afflictions to weak planets becoming indicators of marriage cause marriage problems.

The functional malefic planets, especially Mars, the lord of the sixth house or Ketu forming relationship either with the ascendant, the seventh or second or fourth house or their lords make the native aggressive and ill-tempered if the benefic influence of strong functional benefic planets is absent. Rahu or Ketu joining hands closely with the functional malefic planet, Mars, make the native/spouse stray and that becomes the reason for the discord. The selfish nature of any of the married partners is governed by the weakness of Jupiter. The debilitated planets in second house close to the most effective point or the lord of the second in debilitation also indicate marital discord.

The marital discord has two dimensions: a peaceful separation/ divorce or quarrels/disputes followed by criminal law-suits. The separations and loss of happy married life are caused by the functional malefic planets whenever they closely influence the house(s) signifying marriage and/or the determinant planet(s) and/ or the significator planet(s). When such a planetary relationship/

influence is developed by the involvement of the lord of the sixth house or the lords of the ascendant, second, fourth, seventh, eighth or twelfth house joining the sixth house start operating, disputes leading to criminal law-suits followed by divorce start.

Let us discuss the matter further through some case studies:

CHART 22

Male born 10th April, 1948, 0402 Hrs. at New Delhi, India.

Me 8°16'
Su 26°50'
Mo 1°19'
Ra 20°57'
12
10
1
As 13°21'
9
Ju 5°45'
11
Ve 12°25' 2
8
5
3
7
Ke 20°57'
4
6
SaR 22°40'
Ma 25°43'

Me 8°16' Su 26°50'	Mo 1°19' Ra 20°57'	Ve 12°25'	
As 13°21'			SaR 22°40' Ma 25°43'
Ju 5°45'		Ke 20°57'	

The sign Aquarius rises in the ascendant. Rahu, Ketu, the Moon and Mercury become functional malefic planets. The lord of the eighth house is debilitated and placed in the second house. The lord of the seventh house is fairly strong. The lords of the third house and ascendant are placed in the sixth house. The lord of the sixth house is placed in the third house. The planetary configuration of third and ascendant lords in the sixth and sixth lord in third house makes the person quarrelsome, especially when one runs the sub-periods of the planets involved. The native saw the main periods of both the Moon and Mars and saw enormous incidence of disputes in life with all concerned. The placement of the most malefic planet in the second house gave him problems in the marital relationships. The native was also involved in the marital disputes and his marriage ended in a divorce.

CHART 23

Female born 21st January, 1963, 2000 Hrs. at New Delhi, India.

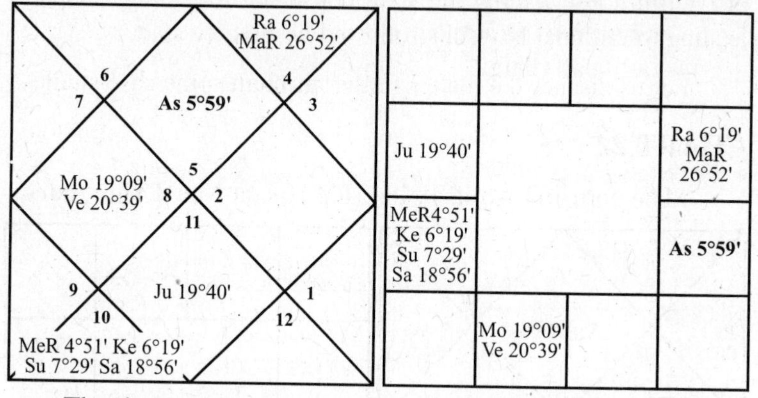

The sign Leo rises in the ascendant. Rahu, Ketu and the Moon become functional malefic planets. Rahu and Ketu are close to the most effective point of the houses of their location and exactly afflict all the houses occupied and aspected besides closely afflicting both the lord of the ascendant and the second house placed in the sixth house. Venus and the Moon are weak as the most effective point of their house of placement is exactly afflicted by the aspect of Rahu from the twelfth house. Venus is additionally weak by being closely afflicted by the most malefic planet, the Moon. The lord of the seventh house is weak as it is combust, badly placed and the most effective point of its house of placement is exactly afflicted by the Rahu-Ketu axis. Jupiter is weak as its dispositor is weak and placed in an afflicted house. Mars is weak as it is badly placed, debilitated, in the state of old-age, has a weak dispositor and the most effective point of its house of placement is exactly afflicted by the Rahu-Ketu axis. There are four planets in the house of disputes which clearly show the incidence of disputes in married life as the lords of the second and seventh houses are also involved. Aiding the negative combinations was operation of the main period of the afflicted Venus. During the sub-period of the afflicted Sun, placed in the sixth house, the marital relationship became inharmonious. The following sub-periods of the Moon, Mars and

Rahu did not favor any improvement. The inharmonious relationship and separation continued. The native, who approached for astrological help, was advised not to go in for a divorce as the natal configurations do not show improvement in any further marital alliance, as well. Therefore, for improving the relationship in the present marital alliance, she was suggested remedial measures for warding off the evil influences of the functional malefic planets and strengthening of the weak planets besides exercising patience.

CHART 24

Female 12th October, 1962, 2222 Hrs. at New Delhi, India.

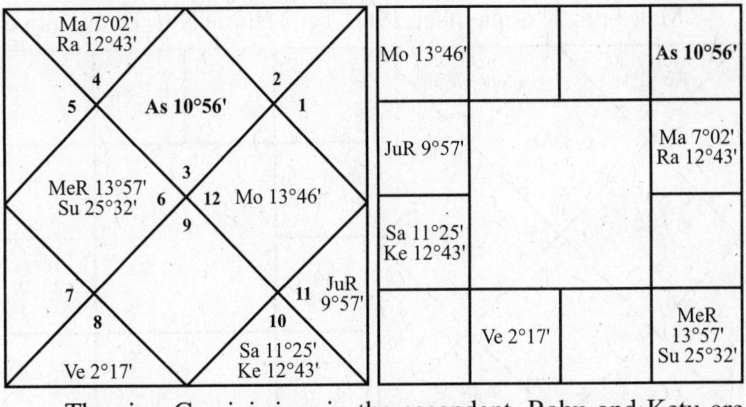

Ma 7°02'
Ra 12°43'
4
5 As 10°56' 2
1
3
MeR 13°57'
Su 25°32' 6 12 Mo 13°46'
9
7 11 JuR 9°57'
8 10
Sa 11°25'
Ke 12°43'
Ve 2°17'

Mo 13°46'			As 10°56'
JuR 9°57'			Ma 7°02' Ra 12°43'
Sa 11°25' Ke 12°43'			
	Ve 2°17'		MeR 13°57' Su 25°32'

The sign Gemini rises in the ascendant. Rahu and Ketu are the only functional malefic planets. The lord of the ninth house, Saturn, is weak as it is badly placed, debilitated in navamsa and is under the multiple affliction of Rahu and Ketu. The lord of the seventh house is weak as its dispositor is weak and afflicted. Venus is weak as it is badly placed and is in infancy. The lord of the second house, the Moon, is weak as, it is afflicted by the aspect of Rahu, it is debilitated in navamsa and the most effective point of its mooltrikona house is under the affliction of Rahu. Mars is debilitated and occupies the afflicted second house. Rahu and Ketu are close to the most effective point of the houses of their location and afflict all the houses occupied and aspected. Mercury, the lord of the fourth house, is under the special affliction of Ketu from the eighth house. Besides the above mentioned afflictions to the planets, the affliction to the most effective points of the second, fourth, eighth and twelfth houses caused disturbance in marital relationship and resulted in a serious marital discord. During the sub-period of Mars, the inharmonious relationship started which was aggravated in the sub-period of Rahu in the main period of Ketu. During the sub-period of the weak lord of the seventh house, the divorce proceedings were started which were finalized in the sub-period of Saturn.

CHART 25

Male born 5th September, 1960, 1643 Hrs. at New Delhi, India.

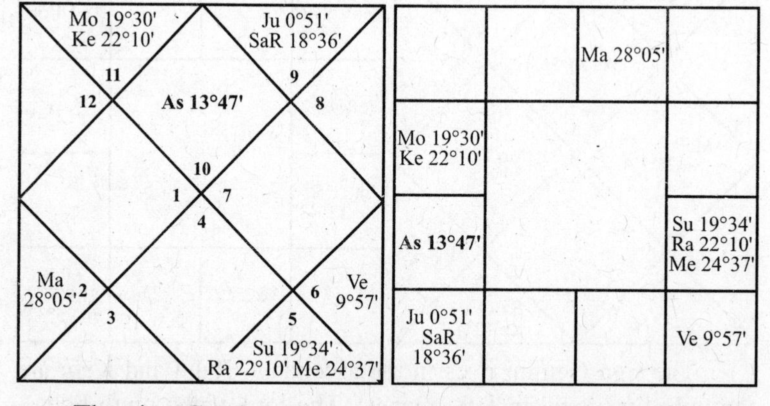

The sign Capricorn rises in the ascendant. Rahu, Ketu, the Sun and Jupiter become functional malefic planets. The lord of the second house is weak as it is badly placed and its dispositor is weak. The lord of the ninth house, dispositor of Venus, is weak as it is badly placed and combust. The lord of the seventh house, the Moon, is weak as its dispositor is weak and it is exactly afflicted by the most malefic planet, the Sun, from the eighth house. The lords of the seventh, eighth, ninth and second houses are closely afflicted by the close conjunction/aspect of Rahu/Ketu. Venus, the significator for wife, is weak as it is debilitated and its dispositor is weak and afflicted. Since in this chart the determinants of marriage and the significator of marriage are all weak and some of them are also afflicted, the problems of inharmonious relations started right from the beginning of the sub-period of Venus, in the main period of Saturn. In the following sub-period of the afflicted Sun, the behavior of the wife went from bad to worse. The divorce took place in the sub-period of Rahu which causes multiple and grave afflictions in the chart. Whenever a particular significator is in its sign of debilitation, the concerned relations fail to fulfill the aspirations of the native.

CHART 26

Male born 1st October, 1959, 0700 Hrs. at New Delhi, India.

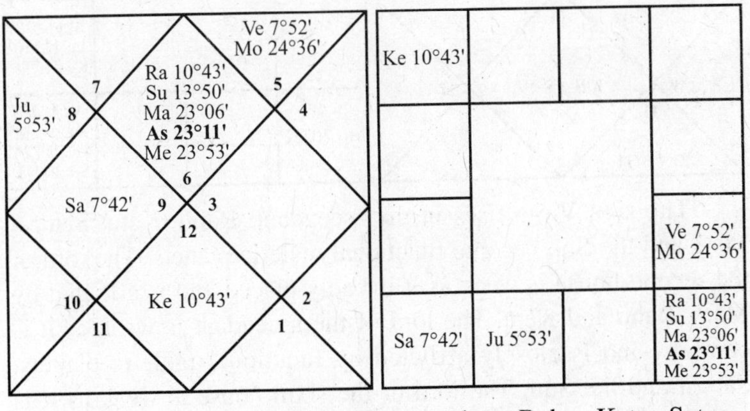

Ve 7°52'
Mo 24°36'
Ra 10°43'
Su 13°50'
Ma 23°06'
As 23°11'
Me 23°53'
7 5
Ju 5°53' 8 4
6
Sa 7°42' 9 3
12
10 Ke 10°43' 2
11 1

Ke 10°43'			
			Ve 7°52' Mo 24°36'
Sa 7°42'	Ju 5°53'		Ra 10°43' Su 13°50' Ma 23°06' **As 23°11'** Me 23°53'

The sign Virgo rises in the ascendant. Rahu, Ketu, Saturn, Mars and the Sun become functional malefic planets. The lord of the second house is badly placed in the twelfth house and is weak. Rahu and Ketu closely afflict the lord of the twelfth house. The most malefic planet, Mars, exactly afflicts the house occupied and houses aspected besides exactly afflicting the lord of the ascendant. The Moon is weak as it is badly placed, debilitated in navamsa and its dispositor is weak and afflicted. The lord of the sixth house occupies the fourth house. In view of the weakness of the lord of the second house and the exact afflictions of Mars to the most effective points of various houses connected with marital affairs, the length of married life was cut short for a period of four months only. The divorce took place immediately after the marriage, in the sub-period of Rahu in its own main period.

CHART 27

Male born 8th October, 1951, 0455 Hrs. at New Delhi, India.

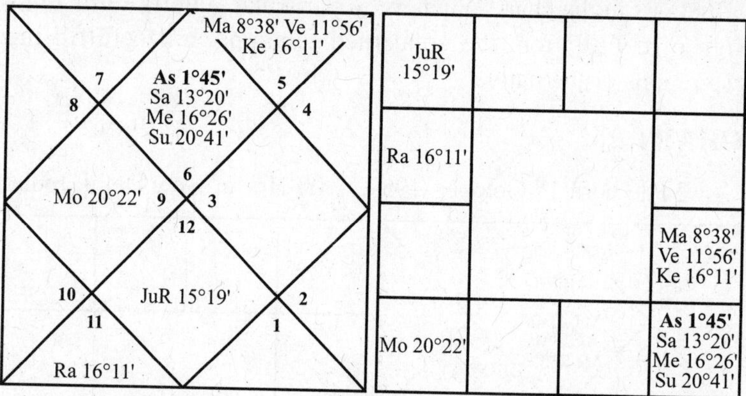

The sign Virgo rises in the ascendant. Rahu, Ketu, Saturn, Mars and the Sun become functional malefic planets. The lord of the second house is weak as it is badly placed and is afflicted by Mars, Rahu and Ketu. The lord of the ascendant is weak as it is combust and is closely afflicted by functional malefic planets, Saturn and the Sun. The lord of the sixth house is weak as it is combust. The Moon and Jupiter are strong in the chart. The native got married during the sub-period of Saturn in the main period of Mars, at the age of 30 years. In spite of all efforts of the native to keep the wife pleased with all types of material comforts and possessions, the relations remained inharmonious from the very beginning due to the operation of the sub-period of the sixth lord. The disputes aggravated in the sub-period of Ketu and the wife deserted the native with a permanent separation. The divorce proceedings were initiated towards the end of the sub-period of Venus in the main period of Rahu. Rahu is placed in the sixth house.

CHART 28

Female born 5th May, 1959, 1203 Hrs. at Ludhiana, India.

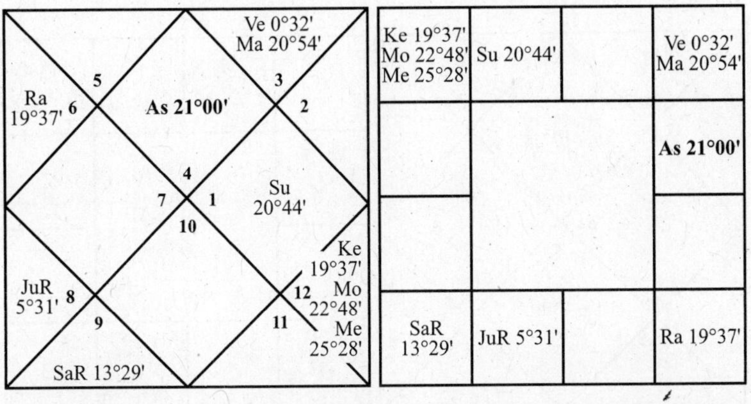

Ve 0°32' Ma 20°54'
5
3
Ra 19°37' 6
As 21°00'
2
4
7
1
Su 20°44'
10
Ke 19°37'
JuR 5°31' 8
12 Mo 22°48'
9
11 Me 25°28'
SaR 13°29'

Ke 19°37' Mo 22°48' Me 25°28'	Su 20°44'		Ve 0°32' Ma 20°54'
			As 21°00'
SaR 13°29'	JuR 5°31'		Ra 19°37'

The sign Cancer rises in the ascendant. Rahu, Ketu, Jupiter and Saturn become functional malefic planets. The lord of the eighth house, ruling the marital tie is placed in the house of disputes. Rahu closely aspects the most effective point of the seventh house and afflicts the same. The lord of the fourth house, Venus, is weak as it is in infancy and is badly placed. The lord of the third house, Mercury, is weak as it is debilitated and placed in an afflicted house. As Mercury is dispositor of Rahu, which afflicts the seventh house, the impact of Rahu becomes more serious. Mars, the dispositor of the Sun, is weak as it is badly placed. The lord of the second house, the Sun, is weak as it is debilitated in navamsa and its dispositor is weak. The weakness of the lords of the second, fourth and eighth houses, affliction to the most effective point of the seventh house and the placement of the lord of the eighth house in the sixth house clearly indicate disputes in married life. The marital discord started during the sub-period of Rahu in the main period of Venus and separation took place in the sub-period of Saturn. The divorce took place in the sub-period of Mercury in the main period of Venus.

CHART 29

Female born 14th November, 1954, 1031 Hrs. at New Delhi, India.

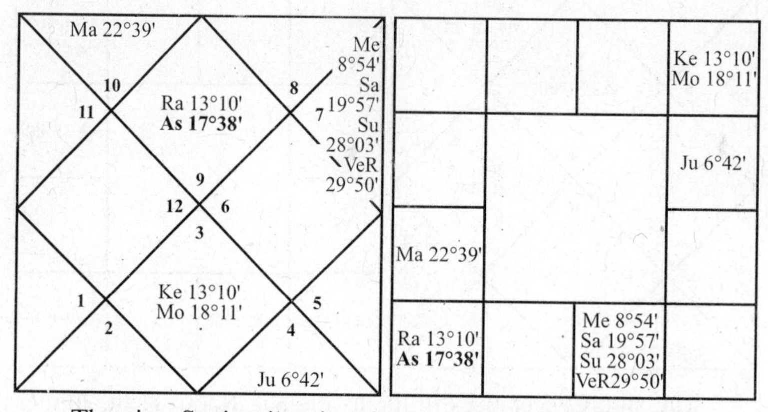

The sign Sagittarius rises in the ascendant. Rahu, Ketu and the Moon become functional malefic planets. The most effective point of the seventh house is severely afflicted by the exact conjunction of the most malefic planet, the Moon, and the malefic influence of the Rahu-Ketu axis, which makes the seventh house very weak. The prime determinant of marriage, the Moon becomes weak, as the most effective point of its house of placement is exactly afflicted by itself. The Sun is weak as it is debilitated and in old-age. Venus is very weak as it is almost exactly combust and in extreme old-age. Jupiter, the lord of the ascendant, is weak as it is badly placed, its dispositor is weak and the most effective point of its mooltrikona house is exactly afflicted by the Moon. Mercury is weak as its dispositor is weak. Mercury is also afflicted by the functional malefic planet, Ketu. Saturn is weak as it is combust and its dispositor is weak. Mars is weak as it is debilitated in navamsa. The severe afflictions to the most effective point of the seventh house and the simultaneous weakness of the prime determinant of marriage, the significator of husband and the significator of marriage resulted into a marital discord. The husband abandoned the native and remarried without even a formal divorce. The native is living with her parents.

CHART 30

Female born 10th October, 1945, 2230 Hrs. at Sargodha, India.

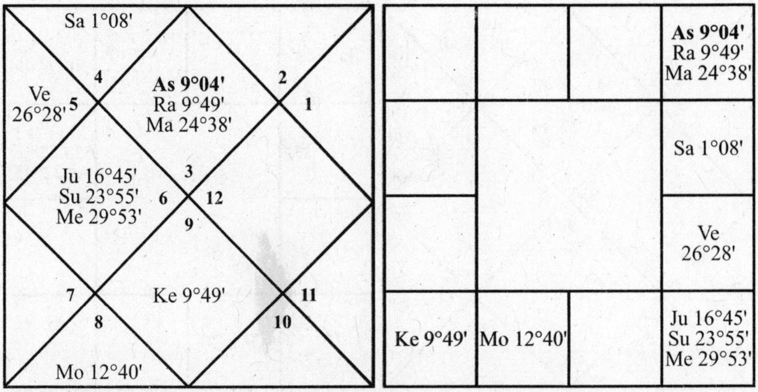

Sa 1°08'
4
Ve 26°28' 5
As 9°04'
Ra 9°49'
Ma 24°38'
2
1
Ju 16°45'
Su 23°55'
Me 29°53'
6
3
12
9
7
Ke 9°49'
11
8
10
Mo 12°40'

			As 9°04' Ra 9°49' Ma 24°38'
			Sa 1°08'
			Ve 26°28'
Ke 9°49'	Mo 12°40'		Ju 16°45' Su 23°55' Me 29°53'

The sign Gemini rises in the ascendant. Rahu and Ketu are the functional malefic planets. Rahu and Ketu are on the most effective point of the houses of their location and exactly afflict all the houses occupied and aspected. The lord of the fourth house is both combust and in extreme old-age and hence very weak. The lord of the second house, ruling family life, is debilitated and badly placed in the sixth house signifying disputes. The lord of the seventh house and significator for husband is also weak as it is combust, its dispositor is weak and the most effective point of its mooltrikona house is exactly afflicted by the Rahu-Ketu axis. Venus, the significator of marriage, is weak as it is in old-age, its dispositor is weak and the most effective points of its house of placement and its mooltrikona house are exactly afflicted by Ketu and Rahu, respectively. The simultaneous weakness of all the determinants and significators of marriage resulted in delayed marriage and inharmonious marital relationships. The marriage of the native saw an end during the main period of Venus and the sub-period of Jupiter.

CHART 31

Female born 22nd June, 1966, 0900 Hrs. at New Delhi, India.

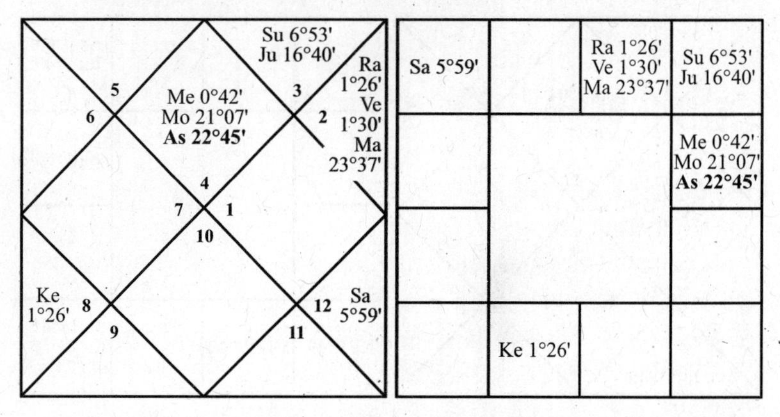

The sign Cancer rises in the ascendant. Rahu, Ketu, Jupiter and Saturn become functional malefic planets. The lord of the second house, the Sun, is weak as it is badly placed. The lord of the third house, Mercury, is weak as it is in infancy and is exactly afflicted by Ketu. As Mercury rules her initiatives, the affliction to Mercury gives faulty decisions. The lord of the fourth house, Venus, is weak as it is in infancy and is exactly afflicted by Rahu and Ketu. It is also closely afflicted by the most malefic planet, Saturn. Jupiter is weak as it is badly placed and combust. The weakness of two determinants of marriage, the lords of the second and fourth houses, the significator of husband, Jupiter, and the affliction to the lord of the fourth house, which is also the general significator of marriage, clearly show lack of marital happiness. The first marriage of the native ended in a quick divorce in the sub-period of Jupiter in the main period of Venus. The native was remarried in the following sub-period of Saturn, the eighth lord, after performance of remedial measures suggested to her.

Chapter 11

Application of Astrological Remedies

Predicting future is one part of the story in case of Astrology while remedial measures is the essence, which helps us in providing umbrella during rainy days. Astrology offers help in the form of astral remedies. Those who do not want to do astral remedies, there is little which can be done for such people except telling them about the period of suffering or the time to come.

When planets are indicating tragic happenings then people usually do not perform astral remedies to protect themselves against the expected losses and the weakness of Jupiter and the lord of the ninth house is always a contributing factor in this regard. The planetary relationships give results according to the indications in case no preventive remedies are performed.

Indications of time can only be modified with the help of the astral remedies. Until and unless the astral remedies are performed, in our views the extent of the services of the divine science of Astrology is very much limited. Some people believe that those who prescribe astral remedial measures are incompetent to make predictions. We can only pity at their lack of power to understand. Such people forget and disregard Maharshi Parashara, who propounded the theory of remedial measures. The preventive remedial measures provide relief from sufferings while remedial measures after some tragic incidence help in rehabilitation.

The strengthening astrological remedial measures are suggested for all the functional benefic planets even if they are not weak and afflicted in the natal chart. The strengthening measures provide a preventive cover to the planets against their transit weakness. Similarly, the propitiating remedial measures are advised for all the functional malefic planets even if they are not forming close afflictions in the natal chart. The propitiating remedial measures provide a preventive cover for transit and natal afflictions.

The problems in life are caused by weak planets and/or afflictions to them. To help people overcome their problems, the astrologer advises appropriate astral remedies, such as meditation and spiritual practices, color and gemstone therapy, the wearing of a Kavach or a Special Power Kavach (amulet) as a protective shield, and the participation in pujas and yagnas, etc. Therefore, a two-way application of astral remedies is administered after diagnosing the problematic planetary influences in a chart. Firstly, the strength is provided to the weak functional benefic planets. The strength can be provided by various methods, e.g. gemstones, color therapy, Kavach (the protective shield containing mystical numbers of the planets) in an auspicious time. Secondly, the intensity of affliction of the functional malefic planets is reduced through the regular practice of meditation, spiritual practices and offering propitiatory charities concerning these planets. The two-way application helps in reducing the impact of malefic planetary influences to a large extent. The preventive use of astral remedies is much more useful than the curative astral remedies.

Generally, people resort to astral remedies in the end after trying all other therapies ignoring the distinct advantage of preventive diagnostic power of the astrological science. Needless to stress the benefit of preventive medicine / redressal measures as against those of the curative measures.

Whenever practiced with faith and sincerity, the efficacy of astral remedies in terms of immediate results depends on many things including the ascendant and the strength of the natal planets. If the functional malefic planets are more in the natal chart, with multiple close afflictions, and the functional benefic planets are weak, one benefits with lot of delay. For example, the people born in the Virgo, Cancer, Pisces, Taurus and Capricorn ascendants need lot of time for sincere and faithful performance of propitiatory remedies. Then the further factors to be seen are the strength of the sub-period and the transit influences.

For both - curative and preventive remedies - the judicious mixture of the following astral remedies is applied.

GEMS: The empirical studies of our ancients reveal that besides medicines the gems and colors are capable of providing good health and mental/spiritual happiness. The efficacy of the gemstones is recognized by the Ayurveda, the ancient system of medicine.

The importance of time, which means the planetary influences at a particular point of time and at a particular place, has always been recognized since ancient times. The references have been found in the ancient literature. It is also firmly believed that the potency of medicines and its curative power increase when the medicine is administered at a particular time of the day and in a particular season.

To provide strength to the weak natal planets, the divine science of astrology recommends use of gemstones for the favorable planets in an auspicious time.

The strength of the planets is raised through the application of influence of concentrated rays of a particular color of a gemstone, which represents a particular planet.

The gems represent the rays of light peculiar to different planets. The men and women use them for raising the power of planets besides wearing them for ornamental purposes.

Gems can be worn in a pendant in an auspiciously elected time. They are usually worn in a ring in the following fingers:

Ruby in left ring finger;

Pearl in left little finger;

Red Coral in left/right ring finger;

Emerald in right little finger;

Yellow Sapphire in right index finger;

Diamond in right ring finger;

Blue sapphire in left middle finger.

In Chapter 6, we indicated the gemstones and colors ruled by each planet. These are the gemstones recommended to begin use in an auspicious time for particular planets if they are favorable in one's birth chart. The weight recommended for all the gems except diamond is between 4.6 to 4.7 carats. The recommended weight for diamond is 1 carat.

COLOR THERAPY: This is a very potent preventive remedy for epilepsy, mental retardation, psychic problems, etc. and is practiced through the use of favorable colors in the matters of dress and furnishings in one's living room. As each day of the week is ruled by a particular planet, each day we should dress at least one wearable garment of the color indicated for that planet if functional benefic.

These are the days of the week and the colors ruled by each planet:

Sun	Sunday	Orange, Pink, Golden
Moon	Monday	White, Silver
Mars	Tuesday	Burning Red
Mercury	Wednesday	Dark Green
Jupiter	Thursday	Yellow
Venus	Friday	Variegated, Royal Blue
Saturn	Saturday	Black, Dark Brown, Blackish Blue

As per the opinion of experts compiled by a Library in Pittsburgh, the grey color of cars was found to be the worst in car safety. As per our color therapy, we had always been suggesting to avoid grey colors by those desirous of happy living and good health.

Kavach: This is a protective shield in the form of a yantra which is made of silver containing mystical numbers of the functional benefic planets in a nativity and is a strengthening measure, providing protection to the natal and transit afflictions of the weak functional benefic planets. With its use, the weak planets are enabled to protect and promote their significations. The Kavach draws its power from the powerful planetary position in which it is created and it is worn also in a specially elected auspicious time for generating the desired impact. It is certainly not a miraculous or magical object. This is part of faith healing and its effectiveness and the amount of help cannot be measured in a scientific manner. The confidence of the Kavach providers is based on the feedback of the users in the last twenty years across the world. This is used both for preventive and curative purposes, and dispenses with the necessity of wearing different gems for different planets.

As we have said, it should begin to be worn in another auspiciously elected time. The auspicious time is worked out with reference to the place of stay. Gem therapy has no comparison to the benefits gained by wearing the Kavach which also acts as a protective shield. When used as a preventive therapy with simultaneous performance of recommended propitiatory (peace making remedies), it is likely to benefit in the following areas:-

- Success in studies
- Success in professional career/business
- Develops leadership skills
- Improves memory and analytical skills
- Protects health against dreaded diseases like cancer, blood pressure, renal disorders, diabetes, epilepsy, paralysis, depression, etc. etc.
- Gives timely marriage
- Gives success in relationships
- Blesses with children

Blesses with achievements and recognition in life and so on and so forth the list is very long.

For further detailed study on election of auspicious time the interested readers may study our book, Systems' Approach For Interpreting Horoscopes.

Vastu: Again this is a preventive as well as a curative therapy for solving the problems in physical and spiritual areas. Wider applications of this therapy are in the field of success of professional ventures. This is practiced through the use of proper outlay of a building to derive geo-magnetic forces for properly energizing the total impact of that building with the help of light, air, space and aura conducive to the main function of the environment.

The relevance of vastu has been discussed in the book, "Predictive Techniques and the Application of Astrological Remedial Measures". The minimum Vastu to be kept in view is:

1. Place of meditation in north east;
2. Bedrooms in south and south west;
3. Children's study in north;
4. Kitchen in south east;
5. Stairs in south-west;
6. Heavy structures in the house in south-west;
7. One should sleep with one's head in east, or south or south west directions;
8. The central place of the residential unit should be empty;
9. There should be openings in east and west and it would be better if the opening is also in south direction;
10. The opening only in south direction creates conflicts and diseases while the openings only in north direction stops family prosperity and sometimes even continuity. Opening only in the west direction brings poverty.

11. The place should be properly lit and pastel colors of functional benefic planets should be used on the walls;
12. The furnishings should be mostly plain or with very little flowery designs. In any case the patterns and designs on the fabric should not be too imposing.

Mantras: As part of the meditation, the recitation of Mantras is prescribed for propitiating the trouble causing planets as per the Vedic rituals.

Charities: These are offered for the functional malefic planets causing afflictions/problems in a horoscope. The malefic influences are effectively tackled with the help of one of these propitiatory remedial measures for each planet when acting as a functional malefic:

Sun:	Serving one's father or helping old age needy persons.
	Give wheat soaked in water with 100 grams of jaggery (Gur) to a cow on Sundays.
	Surya Namaskar at sunrise.
	Observe law of the land meticulously.
Moon:	Serving one's mother or old age women.
	Give dough to a cow on Mondays.
	Keep a fresh water pot for the birds.
	Offering boiled rice with sugar to the birds.
Mars:	Service / help to younger brother(s).
	Prayers/meditation every morning for at least 10 min.
	Being considerate to one's servant(s).
	Exercising patience.
Mercury:	Helping poor students and needy children.
	Donating to orphanages, twice a year.
	Offering green fodder (about 2 Kg) to a cow daily.
	Donating green pulses - every week.

Jupiter:	Offering service to one's preceptor/teacher.
	Prayers/meditation every morning.
	Offering banana in small pieces to the birds.
	Offering one bundi laddu (an Indian sweet) or any yellow sweet to the birds daily.
Venus:	Being considerate to one's wife or helping ladies in distress.
	Donating sugar, rice and cooking oil.
	Offering white sweets to the birds daily.
	Donating silken clothes of bright colors.
Saturn:	Being considerate to servants.
	Offering simple salty food to the birds daily.
	Donating black pulses or salt or mustard oil on Saturdays in a temple.
	Donate to organizations that help poor people, twice a year.
Rahu:	Serving one's parents.
	Give part of your breakfast to the birds daily.
	Donate for old age needy persons or lepers, twice a year.
	Giving away brown colored sweets to the birds daily.
Ketu:	Offering some food to a stray dog.
	Donate for the old age homes, twice a year.
	Prayers to Lord Ganapathi.
	Serving/helping institutions or persons working for spiritualism.

These remedies are to be performed daily in the morning after bath and before breakfast. In case the native is unable to do so as in the case of sickness or out of town or in the case of children, these remedial measures can be performed by parents or spouse. If the offering is not accepted by a dog or cow, another dog/cow should be tried. The remedial measures should be performed regularly and the performance of any one of the suggested measures for a particular planet would suffice.

The weakness of the significator planets, as indicated earlier, is made up with the help of a specially prepared Kavach or a Special Power Kavach to be worn by the native in an auspiciously elected time. For details of the design, size and mystical numbers to be engraved on both sides of the Kavach, the readers may please refer to our book, "Predictive Techniques and the Application of the Astrological Remedial Measures".

These Kavachs get power to do good not only due to the engravings being done in an auspicious time but also due to a prescribed way of life. The person prescribing use of the Kavach should follow these principles:

- Bath in the morning without any bed tea, etc.
- Prayers to Lord.
- Performance of propitiatory remedies as per one's own chart.
- Practice the divine way in life i.e. (1) Be content; (2) Increase utility to humanity; (3) Help poor and needy; (4) Be kind, generous and benevolent; and (5) Avoid deeper involvement in sensual pleasures, anger, pride, greed and envy.

Continuous practice of the above principles helps in generating power for helping others to ward off evils in life and derive benefits indicated by the benefic planets in one's chart.

The simple propitiatory (peace making) remedies are based on Bhoota yagya, one of the five great sacrifices mentioned in Vedic literature and Upanishads, and the planetary tastes and preferences. For further details on application of astral remedies, electing auspicious time for wearing Kavach or Special Power Kavach and FAQs the interested readers may refer to our book, Systems' Approach for Interpreting Horoscopes. For case studies on handling progeny problems, psychiatric problems, marriage problems and financial prosperity through astral or jyotish remedies, the readers may refer to our book, Predictive Techniques and the Application of Astrological Remedial Measures.

Chapter 12

Some Other Important Concepts

Rectification of Birth Charts

The rectification of birth charts is a two way process: Firstly for the rectification of the ascendant; and secondly for the rectification of the ascending degree. While finding out the ascendant is quite easy with the help of the planetary configurations (relationships) developed through close conjunctions, close aspects and placements, the determination of the ascending degree is a lengthy process and sometimes it can take about one year's time after a preliminary hypothesis.

To find out the ascendant:

1. Find out the close conjunctions of planets and see which functional malefic planet is afflicting which other planet or the most effective point of house(s).
2. If the native concerned is suffering on account of the significations of the house containing the mooltrikona sign of the said afflicted planet then the ascendant stands rectified.
3. In case it is not so, then the next or the previous ascendant is to be tried with reference to close relationships of the functional malefic planets or the most effective point of various houses.
4. This exercise is always recommended for the horoscopes where the ascending degree goes from zero to two or three degrees or from twenty eight to thirty degrees. This gives a sound footing for the rectification of the ascendant.

To find out the ascending degree the following process is undertaken:

This is based on the transit of the functional malefic planets over natal weak planets and over the most effective point of the houses where mooltrikona signs of weak planets fall.

First of all, identify the weak planets, the functional malefic planets and the afflicted planets in a chart. Then see the transit position of functional malefic planets with reference to the ascendant over the weak natal positions. Note the houses where the exact conjunction or aspect is likely to be formed with the most effective point in the near future, specially the house(s) having mooltrikona sign of weak planet(s). Keep a watch at what degree the extreme unfavorable results are felt and note down the same for the purpose of rectification. To test whether the degree noted by you is the most effective point of the house you have to repeat this exercise at least twice with reference to the identified degree. If each time on subsequent occasions transit effects of functional malefic planets create unfavorable results at the degree identified, the degree of the ascendant will have to be modified accordingly. Roughly, one degree of ascendant means a difference of three to four minutes in the time of birth. Taking into account this degree of the ascendant and the tentative time, the birth chart will have to be reworked.

This technique is very useful for:

(a) Identifying significant events likely to happen due to exact/close aspects/conjunctions of functional malefic planets with the most effective point of weak house(s)/weak planets.

(b) Identifying significant events likely to happen due to close/exact aspects/conjunctions of functional benefic planets with the most effective point of strong house(s)/strong planets.

(c) To answer queries of recovery from illness.

(d) To answer questions for expected favorable results if exact or close conjunctions/aspects occurring between natal positions and transit functional benefic planets are likely to take place in the near future.

Analysing Capability of Planet to Bless with their Significations

Both the positions - natal and transit - of the planet under impact are to be studied. The planets would be able to bless the native with their significations, both general and particular, if they are strong both in the natal chart and in transit.

Identifying Transit Influences

The result of a particular house will be influenced by a transiting planet when it is near to its most effective point depending upon its functional nature whether benefic or malefic. Considering the triple transit triggering influence, the benefic or malefic impact of transit planets is to be seen on all natal and transit planets, including functional malefics and functional benefics, and the benefic or malefic impact of natal planets is also to be seen on both transit functional malefics and transit functional benefics. The things governed by the planets would be their general and particular significations. Similarly, when the impact is on the most effective point of any house, the significations of the house occupied and house(s) aspected would be influenced by the transiting planet.

Use of Divisional Charts

The divisional charts arc used for judging the true strength of a planet while studying its impact in a particular field. Any planet occupying its sign of debilitation in a particular divisional chart will fail to protect its significations regarding that particular field in its sub-periods.

First of all let us understand what a divisional chart is? A divisional chart is erected by dividing a sign into parts. For example, if we want to prepare a divisional chart for one-ninth part of a sign (rasi), we will divide the 30 degrees i.e. the extent of a sign in nine equal parts of 3 degrees and 20 minutes each. We have a standard methodology for reckoning the signs of natal planets (planetary position as noted at the time of birth) as well as the rising degree of the ascendant in the divisional chart for ninth part, which is known as the navamsa chart. We will not go into the details of preparing the divisional charts here. You can make the divisional charts with the help of the tables 2 to 13 given at the end of this book. We will see the natal sign and degree of a planet and see its corresponding position in the divisional chart. For example, if an ascendant is rising in Virgo 23 degree, its position in decante would be Taurus; in turyamsa would be Gemini; in panchamsa would be Leo; in sapthamsa would be Leo; and so on and so forth. The natal sign is to be read in columns and natal degrees are to be read in rows. The corresponding number reckoned with the help of the column position and row position represents the sign number in the concerned divisional chart.

For detailed analysis of the horoscope, we have to study the divisional charts. These are studied for two purposes. Firstly, we study them to see the strength of a planet by observing its placement in various divisions. If it is placed in its own sign, its mooltrikona sign or its exaltation sign in most of the divisions, it is treated as strong. Its placement in most of the divisions in its sign of debilitation renders it weak. A planet which is weak in the natal chart does not improve its position by occupying benefic, exaltation or own sign in the divisions. However, wearing a gemstone or a Kavach (yantra) in a duly selected auspicious time can strengthen those planets, which are weak but functionally favorable for a person. Secondly, the divisional charts are studied for identifying the results of a particular aspect of life by studying the corresponding divisional chart along with the concerned house in the natal chart. For example, if we want to study the general fortune, we will study the ninth house and the divisional chart known as navamsa (D-IX) along with the natal chart of the person.

From the various divisional charts, we analyse and examine the significations indicated against each:

Hora (D-II)	Wealth
Decante (D-III)	Happiness From Younger Brothers And Initiative
Turyamsa (D-IV)	Net Assets
Shashthamsa (D-VI)	Health And Type Of Diseases
Sapthamsa (D-VII)	Progeny And Happiness Therefrom
Ashthamsa (D-VIII)	Longevity
Navamsa (D-IX)	General Fortune, Marital Happiness And Religious Pursuits
Dasamsa (D-X)	Profession, Fame And Deeds
Dwadasamsa (D-XII)	Parents
Chaturvimsamsa (D-XXIV)	Education

('D' Stands For Division)

For example, if we want to study the professional field, we have to see the dasamsa. If there is no mooltrikona sign in the ascendant of the dasamsa, we consider the position of the prime and secondary determinants of the professional affairs of the natal chart in dasamsa. If the ascending sign of dasamsa is a mooltrikona sign of a particular planet, the same planet is also considered as an additional prime determinant of the profession. For judging the strength of the primary and secondary significators in dasamsa, we have to see if these planets have gone to their signs of debilitation in dasamsa.

A planet which occupies the same sign in rasi and navamsa charts is called vargottamma. Classics indicates good results to planets in vargottamma amsa. But the views of the author are that a vargottamma planet shows favorable results only if such a planet is strong in the rasi chart. Saravali also indicates that "a planet in its own decante bestows good results while the one in own navamsa makes one lucky. A planet occupying its own sapthamsa bestows courage, name, fame and wealth. One becomes devout and helpful if a planet is in its own dwadasamsa." But according to SA, the weak planets in rasi do not improve their strength by being strong in navamsa or other vargas.

The planets are considered weak for all purposes if they occupy debilitated navamsa and are considered weak for specific purposes if they occupy the corresponding debilitated amsa. For example, if any planet is strong in rasi and navamsa, but debilitated in dasamsa, it makes it weak only for the purposes of the 10th house. But being debilitated in navamsa makes it weak regarding all its general and particular significations. Thus the study of divisional charts becomes necessary for clearly delineating the results of the various aspects of life through the identification of the real strength of planets in the D-charts. The accuracy of birth time remains the sole prerequisite for analysing a divisional chart with reliability.

For further detailed study the interested readers may study our book, HOW TO STUDY **Divisional Charts.**

Marital Compatibility

Marital compatibility (MC) has to be seen on the following seven aspects for each person:

1. Health
2. Temperament
3. Sexual urges
4. Marital happiness
5. Longevity
6. Longevity of the marital tie
7. Spiritual development

Health is seen from (1) the lords of the ascendant and/or sixth house containing a mooltrikona sign, (2) the Sun, (3) the Moon, and the placement/strength/affliction of the planets (1) to (3) so identified. All the houses/planets are seen.

Temperament is seen through the influence of the lord of the sixth house containing a mooltrikona sign not only on the most effective points of the houses ruling marriage i.e. the second, fourth, seventh, eighth and twelfth houses but also on the most effective points of the third, fifth and first houses and/or the placement of any of the lords of these houses containing a mooltrikona sign in the sixth house.

Sexual Urges are seen through the influence of Mars, Rahu or the lords of the eighth and/or twelfth houses containing a mooltrikona sign on the MEP and/or lords of any of the houses related to marriage and/or ascendant as they stimulate the urges. Saturn and Ketu influencing deflate the urges.

Marital Happiness is seen through the strength of the seventh, second, fourth, eighth and twelfth houses containing mooltrikona signs. All the houses are seen. Afflictions harm relationships and cause termination of marital tie through divorce or death.

Longevity is seen through the strength of lords of the first, eighth and/or twelfth houses containing a mooltrikona sign and the significator of longevity, Saturn. All the houses/Saturn are seen.

Longevity of the Marital Tie is seen through the strength of the seventh, eighth, second and twelfth houses containing a mooltrikona sign. All the houses are seen.

Spiritual Development is seen through the strength of the fourth, ninth and tenth houses containing mooltrikona sign(s) and the planets the Sun and Jupiter. All the houses/planets are seen.

Examining Marital Compatibility is much more than horoscope matching on the basis of the so-called **Nakshatra** matching only.

Best signs for matching not only among themselves but also with even signs are Aries, Gemini, Leo, Libra, Sagittarius and Aquarius ascendants. If need be the matter may be got analysed through an expert Systems' Approach astrologer.

Pisces, Virgo, Taurus, Cancer, Capricorn and Scorpio ascendants require a detailed matching analysis for marital compatibility and should better not be matched amongst themselves.

Not only the application of preventive astral remedies but also the election of a muhurta (auspicious time) for celebrating the marriage are very important for ensuring a long lasting marital relationship with comparatively more harmony. It makes it possible to match the even signs among themselves.

For further detailed study the interested readers may study our book, **How to Analyse Married Life.**

Manglik

The most dreaded concept of Manglik means early death of spouse or inharmonious relationship with the spouse in the early years of marriage. A native is treated as Manglik when Mars is placed in the first, second, fourth, seventh, eighth and twelfth houses from the natal ascendant or natal Moon. Some modern savants even include these positions from Venus. This way more that 80% of the human beings will be graded as Manglik. This concept is also far from the truth.

The said position of Mars in a chart does not make a native Manglik in case Mars is a functional benefic for the natal chart. For the natal charts where Mars becomes a functional malefic i.e. Virgo, Scorpio and Taurus ascendant charts, it can generate the results of the so-called Manglik yoga if the association of Mars is close/exact to the most effective point of the house and the lord of the house where Mars is posited, is weak. There is no exception to this combination. However, the close trine aspect of a functional benefic

Jupiter and the third aspect of a functional benefic Saturn are capable of warding off the evil results generated by Mars to a large extent.

The functional malefic planets as per the Systems' Approach act identical to Mars in case these malefic planets form close conjunction/aspect with the houses/planets signifying marital happiness. Therefore, for understanding the true impact of Mars in a natal chart we have to clearly understand the functional nature of planets.

For further detailed study the interested readers may study our book, A Complete Book on Triple Transit Influences of Plantes.

Prasna (Horary Astrology)

The prasna chart is made for answering specific questions at a particular time for those natives who do not possess a natal chart or their birth details. The essential condition for efficacy of the prasna chart is that the person coming for prasna approaches an astrologer when one is impelled by one's inner self for seeking astrological help for a specific query. A complete chart like the birth chart for the time and place where the person formulated the question is erected.

For a detailed study on this, the readers may refer to our book, A Complete Book on Horary Astrology.

Frequently Asked Questions

Here, we are taking up some of the points which are often asked by the students to understand the finer details of the analysis of planetary influences through systems' approach.

Is a weak functional malefic planet less evil?

Not necessarily. The quantum of influence of the functional malefic planet (FM) on another planet or most effective point (MEP) of the house is gauged through the closeness of the conjunction or aspect. The afflictions to the planets/houses are caused by the close conjunction or aspect of the FMs in a nativity. Regarding otherwise "strong" planets and/or MT houses, the normal afflictions are effective within one degree range while the special/multiple afflictions are effective within two degrees range, becoming these otherwise "strong" planets/MT houses weak on this account. The normal afflictions to weak planets/MT houses are fully effective if they are within one degree range while afflictions are 80%, 60%, 40%, 20% and 0% if the afflicting planet is having a 1 deg, 2 deg, 3 deg, 4 deg and 5 deg longitudinal difference, respectively, from the weak planet/MEP of the weak MT house. The special/multiple afflictions to weak planets/MT houses are fully effective if they are within two degrees range while afflictions are 75%, 50%, 25% and 0% if the afflicting planet(s) is having a 2 deg, 3 deg, 4 deg and 5 deg longitudinal difference, respectively, from the weak planet/MEP of the weak MT house. It is most severe if the weak and afflicted planets are badly placed. The experience based on the feedback of the people indicates that these afflictions can be taken care of up to 80 - 90% with the help of the astral remedies i.e. special Kavach, gems and charities (peace making remedies), etc. If the planets/houses are strong, the damage is minimum. For non-MT houses, the impact of the affliction is 100% to 0% depending upon the longitudinal difference between the FM and MEP of the house as explained above for the weak planets/MT houses. If a planet being lord of a house is weak one should see the strength of the significator (karaka) and the supplementary houses.

The weakness of the FM is altogether a different aspect and that weakness does not reduce the malefic influence of the FM when it forms close conjunctions or aspects with other natal planets because it acquires malefic nature due to the lordship of a malefic house and not because of its strength or weakness. If a FM is weak, then its general significations and the significations of its MT house are lost or harmed.

Is a functional malefic planet less evil if exalted? Venus in Pisces for Taureans, for example.

The reply to this point, as well, is included in the above question. If the FM does not cause a close conjunction or aspect with other natal positions, then its strength would help promote the general significations of the said planet and the significations of its MT house, which is the sixth house in the case of Taureans. The sixth house rules financial position, health and one's position in the matter of disputes, etc.

Is the strength of planets better when exalted rather than being in their own mooltrikona sign?

The placement in own MT sign is better. In case of exaltation they are dependent upon the strength of their dispositor.

If a functional malefic planet aspects another planet in the FM's own mooltrikona, is that planet afflicted?

Yes. A natal/transit FM never afflicts its own MT house but can afflict all the planets placed there other then itself.

Will the ascendant become weak if it is in the beginning or ending degrees of the sign?

The strength of the ascendant is to be gauged through the strength of its lord, in case it contains a MT sign. The degree of the ascendant does not make it weak or strong. However, if the ascending degree is either in the beginning or in the ending then, sometimes, only weak planets can cause close impact as per their nature on the MEPs of the various houses. And this close impact would only generate hopes or delayed results. But if the planets are strong, they would bestow good results irrespective of the ascending degree even if they do not closely influence the MEPs of various houses occupied or aspected.

Can the transit strength exceed the natal strength of a planet?

No. If a natal planet is weak the orb of transit affliction will remain 5 degrees even if the planet is strong in transit.

Is there ever a time when the transit influence continues for a longer duration?

Generally, the maximum limit of transit influences is around four months when Rahu/Ketu axis is stationary.

Does a functional benefic planet ever cause harm?

The FBs, when strong in the natal chart, never cause any harm. There can be slight tension if during their sub-periods there are some short lived transit afflictions. When the FB is weak, it is vulnerable to get harmed through the natal or transit afflictions caused by close conjunctions/aspects.

For an extensive list of FAQs, the interested readers may consult our book, **Systems' Approach for Interpreting Horoscopes**, or visit Easy Way **To Learn Astrology** at www.YourNetAstrologer.com.

Reasons for Problems in Life

1. Weak planets;
2. Badly placed planets;
3. Afflicted planets;
4. Prolonged transit affliction to weak natal planets;
5. Transit of slow moving planets - Rahu, Ketu, Jupiter and Saturn in malefic houses;
6. Sub periods of functional malefic planets and afflicted planets.

How to Identify Planetary Influences in a Horoscope

1. Placement of planets;
2. Close conjunction of planets with other planets;
3. Close conjunction of planets with most effective point of houses;
4. Close aspects with other planets;
5. Close aspects with the most effective point of houses.

Whenever the lord of the any house containing a mooltrikona sign goes to the 6th, 8th and 12th houses ruling diseases, accidents and losses, respectively, the native has to suffer on account of bad health for the aspects of the health governed by the planet and the house concerned.

Whenever the lord of the 2nd house containing a mooltrikona sign goes to the 12th house ruling losses, this indicates that status in life will not be achieved unless the person moves from the place of birth, possibly to another country.

Rahu's influence on the most effective points of 1st, 3rd, 5th or 10th house and on the planets Sun, Moon and/or Venus gives gambling or speculative tendencies and if at the same time Mercury, ruling analytical power, is badly placed and under the severe affliction of the most malefic planet, the native suffers on account of unmanageable anxiety leading to depression, nervous breakdown, hypertension, insomnia, coronary diseases, etc.

The close influence of the lord of the 8th house during its own sub-period gives various obstructions and setbacks to the significations of the houses and planets that are under its affliction.

The 3rd house and the planet Mercury rules mental and physical growth while the 5th house governs intelligence and the 4th house rules power of grasp and ability of acquiring education. Weakness and/or affliction of the planets connected with the 3rd,

4th and 5th houses and the Moon and Mercury result in mental retardation.

When a functional malefic planet is prime significator of health and is involved in close conjunctions/aspects in a particular chart, its role of functional malefic takes precedence over its role as prime significator of health.

The natal afflictions by the lord of the sixth house and Rahu cause diseases that may respond to symptomatic treatment. The natal afflictions by the lords of the 8th and 12th houses and Ketu cause chronic diseases and if the afflicted planet is very weak, the native suffers from fatal diseases and may have to undergo surgery, etc.

Every time any otherwise "strong" functional malefic planet afflicts exactly the most effective point of its house of placement containing any sign other than its mooltrikona sign, it becomes weak for that reason. When the affliction is special or multiple, the orb of affliction can extend to two degrees.

In case of mutual influence between a functional malefic planet and a functional benefic planet, the predominant impact is that of the functional malefic planet both in the sub-periods of the functional malefic planet and the functional benefic planet.

The problems are always concerning the weak planets or the sub-periods of the functional malefic planets for trend results related to sub-periods. The short-term problems are indicated by the influences of transit or natal functional malefic planets over weak natal or transit planets. The good results should be indicated for the significations of the strong planets having benefic close conjunctions or aspects.

A functional benefic planet's position in any of the malefic houses makes it weak but if it is in the eighth house near the most effective point of the house, then despite weakness it is good as it aspects the most effective point of the second house.

Chapter 13

Conclusion

Let us, first of all congratulate you for going through the concepts and knowledge of this divine science for understanding the meaning of your life, removing strains of uncertainty and developing capabilities for guiding others in situations of confusions and uncertainties. You have been exposed to various concepts, preparation of a horoscope, tools for studying a horoscope and illustrations for identifying some of the areas of human life. The system remains same for analyzing other aspects of life. You have to identify the concerned houses, their lords, significators and the divisional charts for identifying any of the events of life. Thereafter you have to proceed with analysis as per Systems' Approach brought out in Chapter 10.

The various aspects of life are governed by the houses, their lords and the planets acting as significators of the particular aspect of life. Sometimes, the first house signifying a particular aspect may not contain a mooltrikona sign. In such a case there may be subsequent MT house(s) and/or planets from where we can identify this particular aspect of life. Therefore, in the end of the book, the appendix 'Order of Seeing Significations' has been added. The readers may refer to the same.

For further studies and for more illustrations you may study our following books:

1. Systems' Approach for Interpreting Horoscopes
2. How to Study Divisional Charts

3. Predictive Techniques and the application of Astrological Remedial Measures

4. Impact of Ascending Zodiac Signs

5. Triple Transit Influence of Planets

The study of these books will surely give you competency and confidence of deciphering the coded messages of the Almighty through the natal chart.

Though lot of confusions, contradictions and inconsistencies are prevailing in the astrological literature, we are sure you will steer clear of these without any difficulty. For sharpening your skills you may go through the charts of the people around you, whom you know well, and continue your study further based on the Systems' Approach. You will realize how close you are to the nerve of this science.

The authors will feel rewarded for their efforts and contributions if an army of competent astrologers comes up for the service of the mankind.

Chapter 14

Some Useful Tables

Table 1

Nakshatras and Alphabets for Naming

No.	Nakshatra	Alphabets for Naming			
		Pada 1	Pada 2	Pada 3	Pada 4
1.	Ashvini (0-00-00)	chu चू	che चे	cho चो	la ला
2.	Bharani (0-13-20)	li ली	lu लू	le ले	lo लो
3.	Krittika (0-26-40)	Aa आ	ee इ	u उ	a ए
4.	Rohini (1-10-00)	Ao ओ	va वा	vi वी	vu वू
5.	Mrigashira (1-23-20)	ve वे	vo वो	ka का	kee की
6.	Ardra (2-06-40)	ku कू	gha घ	da ड	chha छ
7.	Punarvasu (2-20-00)	ke के	ko को	ha हा	hee ही
8.	Pushya (3-03-20)	hu हू	he हे	ho हो	da डा
9.	Ashlesha (3-16-40)	dee डी	du डू	day डे	do डो
10.	Magha (4-00-00)	ma मा	mi मी	mu मू	may मे
11.	Purvaphalguni (4-13-20)	mo मो	ta टा	tee टी	(tu) too टू
12.	Uttaraphalguni (4-26-40)	tay टे	to टो	pa पा	pee पी
13.	Hasta (5-10-00)	pu पू	sha ष	na ण	tha ठ
14.	Chitra (5-23-20)	pay पे	po पो	ra रा	ree री
15.	Swati (6-06-40)	ru रू	re रे	ro रो	ta ता
16.	Vishakha (6-20-00)	tee ती	tu तू	tay ते	tao तो
17.	Anuradha (7-03-20)	na ना	nee नी	nu नू	nay ने
18.	Jyeshtha (7-16-40)	no नो	ya या	yee यी	yu यू
19.	Mula (8-00-00)	ye ये	yo यो	baa बा	bee बी
20.	Purvashadha (8-13-20)	bhu भू	dha धा	pha फा	dhaa ढा
21.	Uttarashadha (8-26-40)	bay बे	bo बो	ja जा	jee जी

22.	Shravana (9-10-00)	khee खी	khu खू	khay खे	kho खो
23.	Dhanishtha (9-23-20)	ga गा	gee गी	gu गू	gay गे
24.	Shatabhisha (10-06-40)	go गो	sa सा	see सी	su सू
25.	P.Bhadrapada (10-20-00)	say से	so सो	da दा	dee दी
26.	U.Bhadrapada (11-03-20)	du दु	tha थ	jha झ	ana अं
27.	Revati (11-16-40)	day दे	do दो	cha चा	chee ची

Notes:

1. The longitudes mentioned under the names of Nakshatras are the starting point of the Nakshatra and extend to 13°20' in each case. Each Nakshatra is subdivided in four parts or padas of 3°20' each.

2. Sanskrit alphabets exist for each pada. These are used for naming a person as per his/her birth Nakshatra.

Table 2 - Hora

Planets in Sign

Long of Planets	Aries	Taur	Gemi	Canc	Leo	Virg	Libr	Scor	Sagi	Capri	Aqua	Pisc
0° to 15°	Sun	Moon	Sun	Moon	Sun	Moon	Sun	Moon	Sun	Moon	Sun	Moon
15°+ to 30°	Moon	Sun	Moon	Sun	Moon	Sun	Moon	Sun	Moon	Sun	Moon	Sun

Table 3 - Decante

Planets in Sign

Long of Planets	Aries	Taur	Gemi	Canc	Leo	Virg	Libr	Scor	Sagi	Capri	Aqua	Pisc
1° to 10°	1	2	3	4	5	6	7	8	9	10	11	12
10°+ to 20°	5	6	7	8	9	10	11	12	1	2	3	4
20°+ to 30°	9	10	11	12	1	2	3	4	5	6	7	8

Table 4 - Turyamsa

Planets in Sign

Long of Planets	Aries	Taur	Gemi	Canc	Leo	Virg	Libr	Scor	Sagi	Capri	Aqua	Pisc
0° to 7°-30'	1	2	3	4	5	6	7	8	9	10	11	12
7°-30'+ to 15°	4	5	6	7	8	9	10	11	12	1	2	3
15°+ to 22°-30'	7	8	9	10	11	12	1	2	3	4	5	6
22°-30'+ to 30°	10	11	12	1	2	3	4	5	6	7	8	9

Table 5 - Panchamsa

Planets in Sign

Long Upto	Aries	Taur	Gemi	Canc	Leo	Virg	Libr	Scor	Sagi	Capri	Aqua	Pisc
6°	1	6	11	4	9	2	7	12	5	10	3	8
12°	2	7	12	5	10	3	8	1	6	11	4	9
18°	3	8	1	6	11	4	9	2	7	12	5	10
24°	4	9	2	7	12	5	10	3	8	1	6	11
30°	5	10	3	8	1	6	11	4	9	2	7	12

Table 6 - Shashthamsa

Planets in Sign

Long Upto	Aries	Taur	Gemi	Canc	Leo	Virg	Libr	Scor	Sagi	Capri	Aqua	Pisc
5°	1	7	1	7	1	7	1	7	1	7	1	7
10°	2	8	2	8	2	8	2	8	2	8	2	8
15°	3	9	3	9	3	9	3	9	3	9	3	9
20°	4	10	4	10	4	10	4	10	4	10	4	10
25°	5	11	5	11	5	11	5	11	5	11	5	11
30°	6	12	6	12	6	12	6	12	6	12	6	12

Table 7 - Sapthamsa

Planets in Sign

Long Upto	Aries	Taur	Gemi	Canc	Leo	Virg	Libr	Scor	Sagi	Capri	Aqua	Pisc
4°-17'	1	8	3	10	5	12	7	2	9	4	11	6
8°-34'	2	9	4	11	6	1	8	3	10	5	12	7
12°-51'	3	10	5	12	7	2	9	4	11	6	1	8
17°-8'	4	11	6	1	8	3	10	5	12	7	2	9
21°-25'	5	12	7	2	9	4	11	6	1	8	3	10
25°-42'	6	1	8	3	10	5	12	7	2	9	4	11
30°	7	2	9	4	11	6	1	8	3	10	5	12

Table 8 - Ashthamsa

Planets in Sign

Long Upto	Aries	Taur	Gemi	Canc	Leo	Virg	Libr	Scor	Sagi	Capri	Aqua	Pisc
3°-45'	1	9	5	1	9	5	1	9	5	1	9	5
7°-30'	2	10	6	2	10	6	2	10	6	2	10	6
11°-15'	3	11	7	3	11	7	3	11	7	3	11	7
15°	4	12	8	4	12	8	4	12	8	4	12	8
18°-45'	5	1	9	5	1	9	5	1	9	5	1	9
22°-30'	6	2	10	6	2	10	6	2	10	6	2	10
26°-15'	7	3	11	7	3	11	7	3	11	7	3	11
30°	8	4	12	8	4	12	8	4	12	8	4	12

Table 9 - Navamsa

Planets in Sign

Long Upto	Aries	Taur	Gemi	Canc	Leo	Virg	Libr	Scor	Sagi	Capri	Aqua	Pisc
3°20'	1	10	7	4	1	10	7	4	1	10	7	4
6°40'	2	11	8	5	2	11	8	5	2	11	8	5
10°	3	12	9	6	3	12	9	6	3	12	9	6
13°20'	4	1	10	7	4	1	10	7	4	1	10	7
16°40'	5	2	11	8	5	2	11	8	5	2	11	8
20°	6	3	12	9	6	3	12	9	6	3	12	9
23°20'	7	4	1	10	7	4	1	10	7	4	1	10
26°40'	8	5	2	11	8	5	2	11	8	5	2	11
30°	9	6	3	12	9	6	3	12	9	6	3	12

Table 10 - Dasamsa

Planets in Sign

Long Upto	Aries	Taur	Gemi	Canc	Leo	Virg	Libr	Scor	Sagi	Capri	Aqua	Pisc
3°	1	10	3	12	5	2	7	4	9	6	11	8
6°	2	11	4	1	6	3	8	5	10	7	12	9
9°	3	12	5	2	7	4	9	6	11	8	1	10
12°	4	1	6	3	8	5	10	7	12	9	2	11
15°	5	2	7	4	9	6	11	8	1	10	3	12
18°	6	3	8	5	10	7	12	9	2	11	4	1
21°	7	4	9	6	11	8	1	10	3	12	5	2
24°	8	5	10	7	12	9	2	11	4	1	6	3
27°	9	6	11	8	1	10	3	12	5	2	7	4
30°	10	7	12	9	2	11	4	1	6	3	8	5

Table 11 - Ekadasamsa

Planets in Sign

Long Upto	Aries	Taur	Gemi	Canc	Leo	Virg	Libr	Scor	Sagi	Capri	Aqua	Pisc
2°43'	12	1	2	3	4	5	6	7	8	9	10	11
5°27'	11	12	1	2	3	4	5	6	7	8	9	10
8°10'	10	11	12	1	2	3	4	5	6	7	8	9
10°54'	9	10	11	12	1	2	3	4	5	6	7	8
13°38'	8	9	10	11	12	1	2	3	4	5	6	7
16°21'	7	8	9	10	11	12	1	2	3	4	5	6
19°5'	6	7	8	9	10	11	12	1	2	3	4	5
21°49'	5	6	7	8	9	10	11	12	1	2	3	4
24°32	4	5	6	7	8	9	10	11	12	1	2	3
27°16'	3	4	5	6	7	8	9	10	11	12	1	2
30°	2	3	4	5	6	7	8	9	10	11	12	1

Table 12 - Dwadasamsa

Planets in Sign

Long Upto	Aries	Taur	Gemi	Canc	Leo	Virg	Libr	Scor	Sagi	Capri	Aqua	Pisc
2°30'	1	2	3	4	5	6	7	8	9	10	11	12
5°	2	3	4	5	6	7	8	9	10	11	12	1
7°30'	3	4	5	6	7	8	9	10	11	12	1	2
10°	4	5	6	7	8	9	10	11	12	1	2	3
12°30'	5	6	7	8	9	10	11	12	1	2	3	4
15°	6	7	8	9	10	11	12	1	2	3	4	5
17°30'	7	8	9	10	11	12	1	2	3	4	5	6
20°	8	9	10	11	12	1	2	3	4	5	6	7
22°30'	9	10	11	12	1	2	3	4	5	6	7	8
25°	10	11	12	1	2	3	4	5	6	7	8	9
27°30'	11	12	1	2	3	4	5	6	7	8	9	10
30°	12	1	2	3	4	5	6	7	8	9	10	11

Table 12 - Chaturvimsamsa

Planets in Sign

Long Upto	Aries	Taur	Gemi	Canc	Leo	Virg	Libr	Scor	Sagi	Capri	Aqua	Pisc
1°15'	5	4	5	4	5	4	5	4	5	4	5	4
2°30'	6	5	6	5	6	5	6	5	6	5	6	5
3°45'	7	6	7	6	7	6	7	6	7	6	7	6
5°0'	8	7	8	7	8	7	8	7	8	7	8	7
6°15'	9	8	9	8	9	8	9	8	9	8	9	8
7°30'	10	9	10	9	10	9	10	9	10	9	10	9
8°45'	11	10	11	10	11	10	11	10	11	10	11	10
10°	12	11	12	11	12	11	12	11	12	11	12	11
11°15'	1	12	1	12	1	12	1	12	1	12	1	12
12°30'	2	1	2	1	2	1	2	1	2	1	2	1
13°45'	3	2	3	2	3	2	3	2	3	2	3	2
15°	4	3	4	3	4	3	4	3	4	3	4	3

Table 13 - Chaturvimsamsa (Contd...)

Planets in Sign

Long Upto	Aries	Taur	Gemi	Canc	Leo	Virg	Libr	Scor	Sagi	Capri	Aqua	Pisc
16°15'	5	4	5	4	5	4	5	4	5	4	5	4
17°30'	6	5	6	5	6	5	6	5	6	5	6	5
18°45'	7	6	7	6	7	6	7	6	7	6	7	6
20°	8	7	8	7	8	7	8	7	8	7	8	7
21°15'	9	8	9	8	9	8	9	8	9	8	9	8
22°30'	10	9	10	9	10	9	10	9	10	9	10	9
23°45'	11	10	11	10	11	10	11	10	11	10	11	10
25°	12	11	12	11	12	11	12	11	12	11	12	11
26°15'	1	12	1	12	1	12	1	12	1	12	1	12
27°30'	2	1	2	1	2	1	2	1	2	1	2	1
28°45'	3	2	3	2	3	2	3	2	3	2	3	2
30°	4	3	4	3	4	3	4	3	4	3	4	3

Bhukti (Sub-Periods)

Planets	Sun	Moon	Mars	Rahu	Jup	Sat	Mer	Ketu	Ven
	D-M-Y	D-M-Y	D-M-Y	D-M-Y	D-M-Y	D-M-Y	D-M-Y	D-M-Y	D-M-Y
Sun	• 18-3-0	0-6-0	6-4-0	24-10-0	18-9-0	12-11-0	6-10-0	6-4-0	0-0-1
Moon	0-6-0	• 0-10-0	0-7-0	0-6-1	0-4-1	0-7-1	0-5-1	0-7-0	0-8-1
Mars	6-4-0	0-7-0	• 27-4-0	18-0-1	6-11-0	9-1-1	27-11-0	27-4-0	0-2-1
Rahu	24-10-0	0-6-1	18-0-1	• 12-8-2	24-4-2	6-10-2	18-6-2	18-0-1	0-0-3
Jup	18-9-0	0-4-1	6-11-0	24-4-2	• 18-1-2	12-6-2	6-3-2	6-11-0	0-8-2
Sat	12-11-0	0-7-1	9-1-1	6-10-2	12-6-2	• 3-0-3	9-8-2	9-1-1	0-2-3
Mer	6-10-0	0-5-1	27-11-0	18-6-2	6-3-2	9-8-2	• 27-4-2	27-11-0	0-10-2
Ketu	6-4-0	0-7-0	27-4-0	18-0-1	6-11-0	9-1-1	27-11-0	• 27-4-0	0-2-1
Venus	0-0-1	0-8-1	0-2-1	0-0-3	0-8-2	0-2-3	0-10-2	0-2-1	• 0-4-3

• Starting Point

Appendix A

Order of Seeing Significations

Under each topic, proceed through the list until you find the house that has a mooltrikona sign. If none of the houses listed have a mooltrikona sign for the ascendant in question, use the first planet listed as the primary significator. It is that house ruler or planet that you come up with that will have primary importance with regard to the signification. Once you have the primary significator, other planets listed become general significators.

Abortions	Fifth and second houses and the planets Jupiter and the Sun.
Accidents	Sixth house and the planet Mars.
Affection	5th House and the Moon.
Allergy	Close influence of Rahu/Ketu and Rahu like planets on weak planets/houses.
Analytical ability	Mercury, 3rd House.
Asthama	3rd House, 4th House, Mercury & Moon.
Assets	4th House, 2nd House, Mars and Venus.
Basic Education	4th House, Moon and Mercury.
Business	Venus and Mercury.
Children	5th House, 2nd House, Jupiter and Sun.
Comforts	12th House, 4th House, 7th House, 2nd House, Sun, Venus and Moon.

Competitions	Lord of the fifth house. Lord of the third house or the lord of the second house if there is no MT sign in the fifth house.
Coronary problems	Exact or very close influence of Rahu, Ketu or most malefic planet on 4th House, Sun and the Moon.
Courage	3rd House, Sun, Mars.
Creative Intelligence	5th House, 2nd House, Jupiter and Sun.
Debts	Sixth house and Moon.
Depressions	4th house, Moon, Mercury and the Sun.
Disputes	Are indicated by the close influence of sixth lord on other planets/houses, planets in sixth house and afflicted Sun and Mars.
Easy Gains	8th House, Jupiter and Sun.
Education (Basic)	4th House, Moon and Mercury.
Education (Higher)	5th House, 2nd House, 9th House, Sun, Mercury and Jupiter.
Education (Spiritual)	9th House, and strength of Sun and Jupiter.
Elder Brothers	11th House and Jupiter.
Employment	10th House, 2nd House and Sun.
Entrepreneurial Capabilities	3rd House, Mars, Venus & Saturn.
Evictions	4th house and the planets the Moon and the Sun.
Family	2nd House, 7th House, 4th House, Venus and Moon.
Fanaticism	Impact of Rahu over the sixth house or that of sixth house and/or nodes on the third, first and tenth houses.
Father	9th House, 4th House, Sun and Jupiter.

Fatal Accidents/ very serious accidents	Eighth house and exact affliction of MMP or Ketu.
Financial Solvency	6th House, 2nd House, Moon and Venus.
Foreign Residence	7th House, 12th House or influence of 7th lord or 12th lord or 9th lord on 4th House or 10th House, Rahu and Venus.
Foreign Visits	9th House, 10th House or influence of 9th lord or 12th lord or 7th lord on 4th House or 3rd House.
General Fortune/ Luck	9th House, 4th House, 2nd House, Sun and Jupiter.
Happy Married Life	7th House, 4th House, 2nd House, 8th House, 12th House, Moon and Venus.
Health (Emotional)	1st House, 5th House, 6th House, Moon and Mercury.
Health (Functional)	1st House, 6th House, Moon and Mercury.
Health (General)	1st House, 6th House, Sun, Mars and Moon.
Health (Physical)	1st House, 6th House, Sun and Mars.
Heart Disease	1st House, 6th House, 4th House, Sun and Moon, Mars, Jupiter.
Husband	7th House, 2nd House, 4th House, 8th House, 12th House, Jupiter and Sun.
Inclinations	5th House, 4th House, 2nd House, Jupiter and Sun.
Income & Gains	11th House, 2nd House, 10th House, 3rd House, Jupiter, Venus and Moon.
Inheritance	8th House, 9th House, 4th House, Sun and Moon.
Initiatives	3rd House and Mars.

Intuition	5th House and the Sun.
Kidney	Sixth house and Venus.
Lawsuits	Sixth house and the planets the Sun and Mars.
Litigation	6th House and planets placed in 6th House.
Longevity	1st House, 8th House, 12th House and Saturn.
Loss of parents	4th and 9th houses and the planets the Sun and the Moon.
Love	Significator is Venus.
Luxuries	4th House, Venus, 12th House and 7th House.
Malignant Tumors	Exact or very close influence of Rahu or most malefic planet on weak planets/houses.
Marital Discord	Influence of lord of the 6th House/Ketu on the weak prime determinants/significators of marriage or the placement of the prime determinants/significators of marriage in the 6th House. The prime determinants for each of the 12 signs in seriatim are Venus, the Sun, Jupiter, the Sun, Saturn, Venus, Mars, Jupiter, the Moon, the Moon, the Sun, and Mercury. Jupiter is significator for husband and Venus is significator for wife and general significator of marriage. These are the significators of marriage.
Marriage Timing	7th, 2nd and 4th houses or the planets influencing these houses.
Marital Tie	8th House, 2nd House and 12th House.
Mental Capabilities	1st House, 3rd House, 4th House, 5th House, Moon, Sun and Mercury.
Mother	4th House, Moon and 9th House.
Musical Talent	2nd and 3rd house, Venus and Mercury.
Nervous Control	6th House and Mercury.

Possesion by spirits	The close influence of Rahu or Ketu on the 5th House, Sun, Moon & Mercury.
Pre-marital Pleasures	Close influence of Rahu or 8th/12th lords on the 1st House, 3rd House, 5th House or 7th House or the planet Venus.
Poverty	Second, fourth and sixth houses and the planets the Sun and Saturn.
Professional Education	2nd House, 5th House and 10th House.
Professional Position	10th House, 2nd House, 5th House, 3rd House, Sun, Mercury, Venus and Jupiter.
Progeny	5th House, 2nd House, Jupiter and Sun.
Prolonged sicknesses	Sixth house & the planets Mars and Mercury.
Prosperity	11th House, 2nd House, 10th House, 3rd House, Jupiter, Venus and Moon.
Purvapunya	9th house, fifth house, Jupiter and the Sun.
Respiratory disorders	3rd House, Mercury & Moon.
Renal disorders	6th House, 7th House and Venus.
Romance	Mars and Rahu.
Short Journeys	3rd House and 9th House.
Speculation	5th House and Mercury.
Spiritual Education	9th House, Sun and Jupiter.
Spiritual Life	9th House, 4th House, Sun and Jupiter.
Sports	3rd House, 9th House, Mars and Sun.
Status	2nd House, 5th House, 10th House, Sun and Jupiter.
Status with Government	2nd House, 10th House, Sun and Mars.

Success	3rd House, Sun and Jupiter.
Tuberculosis	4th House, Moon and Mercury.
Vehicles	4th House and Venus.
Wealth	2nd House. To find the the prime indicator if there is no MT sign in the 2nd house, then one goes to the 4th house, the 9th house and then the 1st house whichever house has the MT sign first.
Wealth giver houses/planets	11th House, 5th House, Moon and Jupiter.
Wealth Accumulated	Venus is the significator planet.
Wife	7th House, 2nd House, 4th House, 8th House, 12th House, Venus and Moon.
Widowhood	Seventh, fourth, second and 12th houses and the impact of MMP/Ketu on these houses.
Will Power	The Sun, 3rd house, lord of first and lord of second houses.
Younger Brothers	3rd House and Mars.

Appendix B

Some Important Concepts and Insights

Prime Determinants

Systems' Approach brought out the concept of alternate planets or houses to be considered in place of the lord of the house where a particular house does not contain a mooltrikona sign. For example, as per classical literature, the prime determinant of marriage was identified as the lord of the seventh house even if it did not contain a mooltrikona sign. But this does not give a correct analysis. As per SA all houses pertaining to marital affairs are considered. These houses are the seventh, second, fourth, eighth and twelfth. The planetary lords of the first two houses of these houses containing a mooltrikona sign are considered as prime determinants.

Under the Systems' Approach, the concept of prime determinants of any aspect of life is considered. The lord of that house (or houses) which contains the mooltrikona sign(s) for any particular aspect of life becomes the prime determinant(s). The various aspects of life may be governed by more than one house. For example the professional matters are ruled by the tenth and second houses. So only that house will be considered as the prime determinant(s) of professional matters which contain(s) the mooltrikona sign(s). In the case where both the tenth and second houses do not contain a mooltrikona sign, then the lord of the ascendant becomes the prime determinant of professional matters. Similarly there are number of houses which rule the marital matters. These include the seventh, second, fourth, eighth and twelfth houses.

So, in addition to the planetary influences on the house, we consider the lord of that house(s) as the prime determinant(s) which contains the mooltrikona sign(s) in the house(s) for studying the aspect of marriage.

Predictive Methodology for House Analysis

The lord of the mooltrikona house, which rules a particular aspect of life, becomes the prime determinant planet for that aspect of life. If the concerned house does not contain a mooltrikona sign then the lord of such a house, which also rules the same aspect and contains a mooltrikona sign, becomes the prime determinant. If no house ruling the particular aspect of life contains a mooltrikona sign, then the significator for that aspect becomes the prime determinant.

Whenever there is a mooltrikona sign in the ascendant of the concerned divisional chart then its lord acts as an additional prime determinant.

When we take up analysis of any aspect of life we consider the following factors:-

1. Prime determinant of that aspect of life.
2. The house(s) pertaining to that aspect of life.
3. Significator of that aspect of life.
4. The additional prime determinant of that aspect of life, if any. It refers to the lord of the ascendant of the concerned divisional chart if it contains a mooltrikona sign.
5. The operating sub period lord.
6. Triple Transit.

The analysis is done through identification of conjunctions, aspects, placements, transits and the operating sub-periods. The closer the conjunctions/aspects are, the higher is the priority for stating the results.

This simple technique leads us to the desired results. When you indicate the areas which are agitating the mind of the person seeking consultation, the person who is seeking the consultation confirms your finding, and seeks remedial measures to come out of the situation.

The case studies in this book are presented for practicing the technique of handling queries. The students have to understand the case studies and planetary configurations in them. They just have to understand the system and they will acquire confidence.

Suppose the most malefic planet is influencing a particular planet or a particular house or a planet other than the eighth lord is placed in the eighth house and its sub-period is running, you can straightaway say that there are obstructions in the significations of the particular planet/house without any hesitation. If the sub-period is not there, even then say in the matters signified by the above referred planet there are difficulties in life.

After narrating the results/indications of afflictions and bad placements, you can proceed with explaining the good placements and strong functional benefic planets. Then concentrate on the prolonged transits of the immediate past and/or the preceding sub-period and prolonged transit influences. This will give you a good start and your confidence level will start getting higher with each and every case study handled. The future is to be explained on the basis of the strength of the forthcoming sub-period lords and/or triple transit influences. Make astral remedies suggestions.

Impact of Prolonged Transit of Slow Moving Planets

Whenever the slow moving planets Jupiter and Saturn are in the fifth, seventh or eleventh houses, the person faces notable problems in the early years of childhood giving setbacks in studies and health. The family also faces stress. This is because Saturn and Jupiter move to malefic houses for prolonged periods in about a year or couple of years. For example when Saturn was transiting Scorpio, it caused multiple health problems, financial difficulties and conflicts to the Gemini ascendant natives during its stay in Scorpio. It also generates the sense of depression. For Aries born natives Saturn's transit in Scorpio caused many obstructions and set backs in their new ventures. For Sagittarian ascendant natives it caused concerns regarding health, expenses, losses and loss of initiatives.

Whenever the slow moving planets Rahu and Ketu are in the ascendant, seventh or ninth houses, the person faces notable problems in the early years of childhood giving setbacks in studies and health. The family also faces stress. This is because Rahu and Ketu move to malefic houses in about a year and half.

During the prolonged transit impact or during the sub periods of afflicted planets of the natal chart the results of medical treatment are very slow or imperceptible.

When the nodes are stationary at the time of birth, the child is vulnerable to congenital defects.

Those born in Taurus, Gemini or Cancer ascendants find the winter season difficult as the fast moving planets pass through their sixth, seventh and eighth houses.

When Rahu and Ketu are conjunct with the most effective points of the houses occupied by them, they make the native vulnerable to sudden and serious illness. This is more so when one or both of them are placed in the malefic houses.

Rahu and Ketu get in an apparent stationary mode after about nine degrees after every three months. Exact position can be ascertained through ephemeral records. Whenever weak, afflicted or badly placed natal planets or the ascending degree is at this stationary degree the person is all of a sudden vulnerable to serious problems for three to four months. So, astrologers need to keep this in mind for their own benefit as well as that of their clients, that special propitiation remedies help. Details for these remedies can be found on our website. To identify the apparent stationary mode after about nine degrees after every three months, the readers can take help from the book, "Sagar's Daily Nirayana Planetary EPHEMERIS 2001 - 2025 (Based on Chitra Paksha / Lahiri Ayanamsa) by V. K. Choudhry," which gives the ephemeral records up to the year 2025.

The regular performance of propitiatory astral remedies reduces the magnitude of afflictions. But the impact of transit affliction lasts till the afflicting planet moves five degrees away. When the planet is transiting in a malefic house, its impact lasts while the planet remains in the malefic house.

Divisional Charts

The divisional charts are drawn by division of houses for specialized analysis of a particular signification; for example, the Navamsa chart is for considering general fortune, marital happiness and religious pursuits in a birth chart. Affliction to the ascendant in a divisional chart by the eighth lord of that divisional chart is as equally serious as the affliction to the prime determinants placed in the eighth house of a divisional chart.

In divisional charts besides the affliction of Rahu and Ketu, the afflictions by the functional malefic planets of the divisional charts should also be considered. However, in a divisional chart the afflictions by the functional malefic planets of the natal chart are not considered. Bad placements are also considered in the divisional charts.

The divisional charts are also used for ascertaining the strength of the prime determinant of a particular aspect of life. In the divisional charts the strength of the following is studied:

i) **the prime determinants of the house of a particular signification in the D-I (birth chart) if they are strong in the natal chart. Those planets which are already weak in**

the birth chart, they do not gain any strength in the Divisional Charts. The strength in the D-1 prevails;

ii) the significator of the particular aspect of life;

iii) the lord of the ascendant of the concerned divisional chart if it contains an MT sign; and

iv) the position of the sub period lord at any given point of time in the concerned D Chart.

The weightage for consideration of a rasi/natal chart is 80% while for divisional charts it is 20%. In some cases the planets are so weak and afflicted in the natal chart that consideration of the divisional chart becomes irrelevant.

For a detailed study on this subject, you can read the authors' book entitled: "How to Study Divisional Charts".

Insights

The afflicting power of the functional malefic planet does not reduce due to its weakness. The afflicting power of the functional malefic planet increases when it is placed in a malefic house or it itself is under affliction.

If the planet/house under affliction is weak, the impact of affliction will be more. The affliction to the MEP of houses is more severe in comparison to the affliction to a planet.

If a fairly strong or a strong natal planet is under the stationary influence of Rahu or Ketu and in transit the said planet is badly placed and/or afflicted, it causes harm to the person.

The weak Moon for those born in the Gemini ascendant gives problems of frequent coughs and colds, seasonal sensitivity and makes them vulnerable to lung and autoimmune disorders.

A weak Venus makes the Taurus born people vulnerable to frequent acidity, constipation and intestinal disorders resulting in headaches to intestinal and liver disorders.

When the lords of the sixth and eighth houses are conjunct or cause a mutual exact aspect, they make the native vulnerable to sudden and fatal mishaps.

Whenever the Rahu-Ketu axis is placed exactly over the most effective points of houses containing odd-numbered signs besides afflicting the houses occupied and aspected, it turns the planets Saturn, Sun, Venus, Mars and Jupiter weak by afflicting their mooltrikona sign houses.

Whenever the Rahu-Ketu axis is placed exactly over the most effective points of houses containing even-numbered signs besides afflicting the houses occupied and aspected, it turns the planets Moon and Mercury weak by afflicting their mooltrikona sign houses.

When a planet aspects Rahu or Ketu, it does not pick up the negative influences of Rahu/Ketu. This is a one way aspect and not a mutual aspect. This is possible in cases regarding special aspects of Mars and Saturn.

If the aspecting planet is a functional benefic planet, then it reduces the malefic and negative impact of Rahu/Ketu. If the aspecting planet is a functional malefic planet, then it increases the malefic impact of Rahu/Ketu.

Prediction of unfavorable results can be/is made for the significations ruled by the weak planets even if there are no afflictions in the natal chart and no planet is badly placed.

The placement of the tenth lord in the second house indicates professional education.

The strength of the Sun, Sun-like houses or planets improve the results of the other planets to some extent.

A short life span is caused by the strong affliction of the MMP (most malefic planet) to the significators of longevity, the placement of planets in the 8th house and an afflicted Moon.

Afflictions depend upon the closeness of the functional malefic planet to the planet/house which is being afflicted.

The placement of the lord of the 6th house in the second house or the lord of the second house in the sixth house creates inharmoniousness or separation in a marital relationship.

Generally, a strong Venus hastens marriage.

A strong Sun brings down the level of sufferings due to afflictions.

The aspect of a functional benefic planet from a malefic house remains favourable commensurate to the strength of the said planet.

When the natal Moon is afflicted by Rahu, Rahu-like planets or is badly placed in the Rahu-like houses the person becomes more sensitive to transit afflictions and especially to unfavorable incidents.

The slow moving planets Saturn, Rahu and Ketu near the most effective point of any house cause serious stress. The slow moving planet Jupiter near the most effective point of any benefic house brings happy events concerning the house transited and the houses aspected.

If a fairly strong or a strong natal planet is under the stationary influence of Rahu or Ketu and in transit the said planet is badly placed and or afflicted, it causes harm to the person.